RADICAL
COMPANIES

WITHOUT BOSSES OR EMPLOYEES

MATT PEREZ, ADRIAN PEREZ, JOSE LEAL

First Edition 2021

RADICAL COMPANIES

Organized for Success without Employees and Bosses

Matt Perez, Adrian Perez, Jose Leal

ISBNs:

Hardcover 978-1-64184-650-9

Paperback 978-1-64184-642-4

Ebook 978-1-64184-643-1

TABLE OF CONTENTS

PART ONE: Our FIAT World

PART TWO: An Alternative to Our Broken Systems

PART THREE: Our RADICAL Company

APPENDICES

Businesses Are Broken and They Break People

This book is about what we call RADICAL Companies, owned and managed by the people who embody them and give them life, it is for people who want to make an impact on the world, not just to make money.

What has evolved into today's economy has worked relatively well for many of us, but has worked best for the powerful few. Without question, things have gotten better since the eighteenth century, but the playing field still tilts to the powerful and deep disparities continue today. By far, the biggest issue is not the wealth gap, but the fact that we accept it as inevitable. It's going to be difficult to do, but we have to shake off those habits that lead us to be so compliant with the way things are.

Today businesses are grounded on imposed hierarchy, fear, and separation. The American and French Revolutions eliminated the ruling royalty, but left the landlords in charge of humanity's wealth. And that's where we've been stuck for a few hundred years.

But we need to move on. People want a place at the table, an equitable share of the wealth they helped create, and a voice on what and how to do things. To make businesses into a positive force for society, we have to turn them into companies that are owned and managed by the people who embody them and make them thrive. Otherwise, we are going to slide deeper into a dystopian nightmare as fewer and fewer people wade in abundance while the rest of us drown in scarcity. We are living better off today but that's only along the financial dimension. In fact, most people alive today live in financial splendor compared with the royalty of previous centuries. On the other hand, we are definitely drowning in scarcity of time and choices. We are definitely stunted in our ability to live a full life, with the ability to change careers at will and not risk starvation in the process. In exchange, most of this wealth is controlled by a handful of people and that's just plain wrong.

This book is *not* about convincing you that there is a problem. If you are happy and satisfied with things as they are, you might want to skip reading the rest of this book. We wrote this book for people who want to live in a more just world than the one we live in today. We wrote it for people who sense that things could be better. We wrote it for those who might have started along one of the many self-management approaches and are looking for what's next.

Rather than complaining about it, or agitating for revolution, or hoping that a benevolent government will rescue us, the change is in your hands. We can help bring about a new paradigm of wealth and well-being, one company at a time. Unfortunately, this effort is not yet focused and it has not generated the impact that we want to see in the world. This book is about helping to concentrate that energy and make a more desirable future happen sooner rather than later.

A Healthy Society

We see companies as places where lots of exploration and experiments will take place. Companies are where people spend most of their waking hours and where they experience what "normal" is. As new habits and new ways of living not driven by fear take root in these companies, they will spread to our families, our schools, our societies, and beyond.

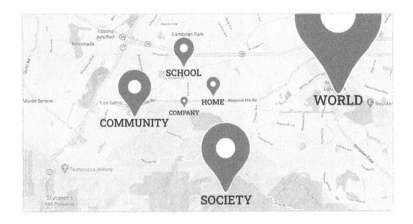

Organization

This book is organized in three parts, starting with, Part One, the story of a self-managed company, Nearsoft, and how it came about.

Part Two lays out the fundamental components of the RADICAL paradigm that will help us move away from the dead end that we are headed towards now.

Part Three lists out a bunch of use cases and examples of what we would do to create a company with decentralized ownership and collaborative management.

Speaking of Authors...

We all came to this point through very different paths.

Matt got to this point after 40 years of working in traditional fiat businesses and more than 14 years at Nearsoft, a co-managed company he and Roberto Martinez co-founded. The experiences he's had along the way, good and bad, underpin this book.

Adrian, like many of his generation, has always been uncomfortable with the because-I-say-so business world. He watched up close how an exciting start up collapsed after the bosses in charge led it down a dead end. In his own startups, he has experienced how difficult it is to make decisions without an explicit alignment mechanism.

Jose started several businesses while in his late teens, rode the Internet wave, and felt the bite of the very same grinder he had helped create. He got off that path and spent several years researching and studying what makes us humans and what prompts us to certain actions and choices. Much of that experience has shaped the work that has gone into this book.

For a longer version of our backgrounds, please see About Us....

Terminology

Throughout the book we use unusual terminology, like the term "fiat," a somewhat obscure term that means the power to give arbitrary orders.

We made up terms, like co-management and put our own spin on co-ownership. We avoid confusing misnomers like "CEO," "executives," and "managers," and euphemisms like "leaders" and we call them all bosses instead.

We even use traditional terms, like company, a bit differently. Terms like "business" or "corporation" are associated with capital while others like "cooperative" and "collaborative" put the emphasis on labor. But the most important element is people, people coming together to create something uniquely human. The very roots of "company" reflect this as it comes from *com-* and *panis* or Latin for a group of people who break bread together. That image is the basis of our story and what's radical about our proposal.

From the Editor

The style of writing could be at times confusing, going back and forth between the "I" and "we."

Unless otherwise stated, Matt Perez held the proverbial pen and the pronoun "I" refers to his own history. The pronoun "we" refers to thoughts and opinions that Adrian Perez, Jose Leal, and Matt Perez hold in common.

PART ONE
OUR FIAT WORLD

1
ONCE UPON A TIME

AS GALLUP, ADP, and others have reported, disengagement at work is extremely high and a good chunk of people's lives is wasted "at work." Businesses know this, but they accept the bare minimum results in exchange for a perception of control.

On the other hand, operating without bosses, or titles, or a ranked hierarchy sounds impossible but it works. I've experienced it at Nearsoft, a self-managed company that Roberto Martinez and I founded in 2007. But self-management is not enough. For a sustainable solution, we need to address the issue of ownership. The static ownership of the past does not work for most of us any more, we need a new model.

Companies are our economic engines. It's easy to understand the frustration that leads to the "fuck the corporation" sentiment, but, honestly, we wouldn't know what to replace them with. Many have tried to turn private businesses into public ones and have the government own them all, but those systems always end up as dictatorships. Decentralized ownership is central to liberty, I know this from my own experience with the alternative. Appealing to "the new man" or our angelical side is not enough, probably because we don't have an angelical side. Or an evil side. Or any sides, we are just people.

Instead, we reimagined companies as places where people learn to manage their work collaboratively, without bosses, instead of today's, "because I say so," FIAT management. Places where people can experience decentralized ownership instead of the FIAT ownership we've inherited from the age of monarchs. We call these places RADICAL companies.

For the RADICAL paradigm presented below, we've tried to keep the things that make modern companies effective at bringing people together and at generating wealth. We've also removed the pieces that are obviously broken and make us miserable and instead point to ways to unlock our voices and spread that wealth according to our contributions.

The Itch

In mid 2005, I started toying with what became Nearsoft,[1] a business to help software product businesses grow their software development teams. By then, I had been involved with six hardware and software startups and I knew that growing an engineering team was getting harder. And it wasn't just me. Many of my peers dealt with the same challenge and we commiserated often.

I was already in my early 50s, so the prospect of looking for "a job" was not very appealing. Lucky me, I knew enough people in the business and could have eventually found a well-paying job with a grand-sounding title but it would be more of the same and I could not get excited about that prospect, so I kept trying to figure out other options.

I was having lunch with a buddy and we commiserated about working with body shops overseas, half a world away. In passing, I said something like, "Doing this stuff on the other side of the world doesn't make sense—but if we could do this in Mexico… that would work great."

Brainworm

As I drove away, the idea of having a team in Mexico kept bouncing around in my head.

I had been outsourcing pieces of software product development to faraway places like India and Eastern Europe because everybody "knew" that it was the way to build products on the cheap. The problem of finding good people came up early and often at Board meetings and their response was predictable, "How about India?" However, I and my commiserating peers knew that it was nearly impossible to make those distant places work when it came to developing software products.

We also knew that it wasn't cheaper, either. Not when you took into account the unavoidable, long, and expensive trips in both directions, and not when you factored in all the rework that resulted from miscommunications and misunderstandings. Cultural differences and language barriers created all kinds of friction. Not being available to speak directly with each other was a killer. You couldn't resolve even simple questions in real time. Instead, a string of emails would fly back and forth, each one getting longer than the previous. Frustration would build up at both ends and what started as a small, simple question would become a major, complicated problem.

And then there was the high turnover. As more and more of us sent work overseas, demand grew beyond capacity and vendors were luring developers away from each other at a very high rate. This meant that the team never achieved a very good understanding of the product, leading to a lot of rework.

The need for finding an alternate source of developers was real. And if we could find them nearby in Mexico...

Opportunity Cost

The issue was not so much the money spent in salaries as it was the cost of lost opportunities. Whenever I found good local developers, money was no problem and we would pay whatever it took to get them to join.

The reason we tried so hard to make those remote places work was in the hope that we could find developers faster and grow our teams a little bit quicker. Otherwise, we could not keep up with customer demands and risked missing the opportunity.

DOT-COM (and Gone)

During the dot-com bubble[2] it became nearly impossible to find software developers or testers or anybody with product development experience. Investment capital was overabundant and lots of new software businesses were springing up very quickly. Developers were getting BMWs as sign-on bonuses! Then, the bubble burst: "On March 10 [2000], the combined value of stocks on the NASDAQ was at $6.71 trillion... On April 6, 2000, it was $5.78 trillion. In less than a month, nearly a trillion dollars worth of stock value had completely evaporated. ... companies were losing between $10 and $30 million a quarter."[3]

Things cooled off after the bust and for a while it became a bit easier to find developers, but that didn't last long. The bust didn't stop software from "eating the world" as Marc Andreesen put it.[4] It barely slowed down its growth back then, and it has accelerated since.

Offshoring

Software outsourcing in the form of offshoring got big in the late 1990s because the year 2000 was going to be a big problem for many organizations. That's because in most cases the year had been saved as two digits instead of four. Storage was expensive back then and keeping half the digits made sense. For example, if your birth year was "1919," most software saved it as "19."

As the deadline approached, Western businesses rushed to fix the bug, popularly called "the Y2K bug," that might bring down their digital systems and their businesses.[5] To do so, they ended up hiring lots of software people in India and a few more in Eastern Europe.

India sounded ideal for that work, with lots of well-educated, English-speaking programmers who were very inexpensive relative to the US and Europe. They would pour over their customers' code and find every instance of "21" and change it back to "1921;" they also had to change any calculation that assumed two-digit years instead of four. By doing so, they would prevent planes from falling down and other cataclysms that were predicted at the time.

Outsourcing morphed to offshoring and expanded from a maintenance function to other aspects of software development. Many big corporations offshored their whole IT operations to third parties in India and Eastern Europe. They saw their IT departments as a cost center and offshoring them at once made them less costly and turned them into a variable expense.

Then, in the early 2000s, even small software product businesses followed suit, with the full encouragement of their Boards, and they started to offshore some of their product development. By 2005, many people had tried it and a few were starting to get disappointed with the offshoring model, including me. What sort of worked for making software for internal use ("you HAVE TO use it, it is your job!"), didn't work so well for making software products ("please, use it, you'll love it").

Cultural friction and big time zone separations were the main culprits.

It Has Legs

As it all came together for me "… in Mexico" became my working hypothesis. But I had a problem: other than the language, I knew very little about Mexico and what little I "knew" about it was all wrong. Luckily, somewhere along the way, I got connected with Roberto Martinez, my future partner.

Like me, my peers in engineering were enthusiastic about the possibility of growing their team nearby, where they could talk to developers any time. And they were thrilled to avoid the cultural friction and the late night and early morning calls. The idea had legs. It would be a welcome service, the market was big, and it would grow as the software industry grew. However, beyond Roberto's and my circle of friends, we would not get far unless we could differentiate Nearsoft from traditional body shops. And the "crazy" Nearsoft culture turned out to be the "feature" that people found most memorable and remarkable. "Mexico" opened the door, our culture closed the deal, and Nearsoftians anchored the relationship for the long term.

Not My First Choice

When I met my future business partner, Roberto Martinez, his company was not my first choice to work with. There were several more mature Mexican businesses that, at the time, seemed to make more sense as partners. I had assumed that partnering with several companies would afford me a faster time to market. These other businesses were more established and already had the staff and the experience. But as I worked with them, they all washed out. Except Roberto's C Cube Technologies.

I realize now that I didn't think of C Cube as my first choice because I was seduced by the traditional marks of success that the other businesses offered. However, it didn't take long to realize that regardless of pedigree Roberto and his team were a better match. The C Cube team was focused on software product development and didn't do anything else. They had worked with US businesses before, and had the right cadence. They were very responsive and transparent. And they were committed to long term relationships, not hit-and-run jobs.

For example, one of the projects we worked on together ran late. I had committed to a fixed price, but I didn't manage well. The client kept changing directions and the project kept dragging. I ended up paying C Cube out of my own pocket and it was getting expensive. I spoke with Roberto and his partner, Julio Gonzalez, about it and without missing a beat they said something like, "We are going to make the client happy, don't worry." The engineer who worked on the project, Rodrigo Yáñez was brilliant. His design anticipated changes that the client asked for much later. We ended up not making a profit, but the client was very happy with the result. They were in fact a good reference for us afterwards. That pretty much nailed my decision to join forces with Roberto and C Cube.

Time Zones

At the time we started Nearsoft, software "outsourcing" and "offshoring" were completely conflated. Whatever you called it, the businesses here in the US wanted to save money, to get more for less. Hire developers overseas for cheap and assign them the easy to do but mind-numbing work. This was a copy-paste of the strategy that hardware manufacturing had followed.

In software, offshoring had worked to correct the Y2K problem. And if it worked for that particular software problem, the thinking went, then it would work for any software development. But the fantasy didn't really work for product development.

Product development is not at all a rinse-and-repeat process. Successful products come from constant experimentation and close interaction with end users to figure out what they consider valuable. It is impossible to write a precise spec for the work to be done. Software product development is an evolutionary process, an ongoing response to its environment. Everybody on the team, including developers, testers, and the product folks, need to talk with one another as problems and opportunities arise. And to do this effectively, they have to be in sync, otherwise differences in the circadian cycle mess everything up. I learned this tidbit at Sun Microsystems, when I was the boss of a group split between Mountain View, California and Morrisville, North Carolina.[6]

The two locations were "only" three time zones apart, but that was enough to throw us out of whack. By the time that the team in California was rolling in, the folks in North Carolina were on their way to lunch. Then, when the Carolinians were ready to get into their afternoon groove, the folks in California were heading out for their lunch.

I took that lesson with me and when we started Nearsoft we only pursued clients that were within one or two time zones of our office in Mexico.

Responsibility vs Authority

Before Sun Microsystems I had worked mostly in smallish startups where taking the initiative was valued and encouraged. Everybody knew that doing so was money in the bank. When I first joined, Sun was still at the stage that taking the initiative was valued. Nine years later, Sun had more than 10,000 people[7] and the culture had definitely taken a turn towards the corporate way.

Most of my time at Sun was in the Graphics & Multimedia side of the house, first in hardware and later in software. We were the supporting cast; the main attraction was the workstation and server folks on the hardware side, and the Operating System folks on the software side. I didn't realize it then, but the supporting cast was a great place to be. We knew our customers, kept them happy, and were free to take the initiative and make decisions big and small along the way. We had responsibility *and* authority (*i.e.*, "we" the bosses, of course).

Then I was made a bigger boss in charge of the Operating Systems team. I had been entrusted with Solaris, the company's crown jewels! It was my "reward" for taking initiative, I thought. But the increase in responsibility came with a decrease in authority. Because it was so central to the rest of Sun's products, everybody wanted to weigh in on every decision related to Solaris. Decisions that would have gone unnoticed in the Graphics & Multimedia side of the house, now became objects of universal concern, scrutinized by all, critiqued and questioned. And often reversed by my bosses.

For example, one of the perennial problems with Solaris was that releases were always late. Every new piece of hardware, every new networking feature, every software library had to go out together on the same release "train." As the train got bigger, the release dates became more and more unpredictable. Departure time was anybody's guess.

There were precious few rules for getting on the train. And what few rules we had were often gamed or outright broken. So we tried to streamline the rules and make them stick.

Very often, new code would "break the build." That is what we called it when new software was added and it stopped the rest of Solaris from working. When this happened, no new code could be added until the faulty code was fixed. We wanted to change this, so we decided that the next time new code broke the build, we would take it out and move it to the end of the line waiting to get on the train. If it was fixed before the train left the station, great, but otherwise, the software train would ship on time. But, hey, the fixed code would be at the head of the line for the next train.[8]

What we had come up with would make releases predictable. But as it turned out, I didn't have the authority to take this kind of initiative. People who had been through this before warned me. The call from Sun's CEO, Scott McNealy, didn't take long,

— Is it true that you told your people to take CODENAME out of the release?

— Yes, it...

— Put it back in the release.

— But their code breaks the build and...

— Put it back in the release. Got that?

— Yes, but it just doesn't wor...

I talked to the people who had warned me and told them about the call. They were deflated by the news, but not surprised. They completed my schooling by letting me know that this also meant that we would have to fix the code ourselves. The featured hardware had already been announced, Solaris had to support it, and it had to go out no matter what. Needless to say, the Solaris trains continued to leave the station unpredictably late, as always.

I lasted less than two years as the Solaris figurehead boss.

I know this situation doesn't sound pretty, but I don't mean it as a criticism of Sun and how it was run back then. None of us knew any different. More than anything, I want to illustrate how in spite of being very innovative in technology, Sun could not innovate itself out of the FIAT hierarchy box that eventually smothered it. If anything, it continued to "go corporate" and eventually faded away.

The lesson I took away from this is that responsibility and authority are essential, not only for working effectively with others, but for the personal feeling of satisfaction. Being responsible for software delivery but having little authority to make changes left me very frustrated. That gave me an inkling of what others must have felt like when I, unilaterally, snatched away their ability to act independently.

The Most Important Lesson

Climbing the ladder of FIAT success at Sun and elsewhere did not come for free. My family, too, paid the price of all that "success." I had climbed up the proverbial ladder, grabbed power whenever I had the chance, and wielded the double-edged sword of fear. All while navigating the corporate moral maze and the ethical traps along the way.[9] I could not help but bring a lot of these terrible habits and stress home with me every night.

In *Rehumanizing the Workplace*, Chuck Blakeman points out that "… management is… unadulterated codependence… Managers are enablers."[10] At home I was the enabler dad, much like I behaved at work. I was inflexible ("because I said so"), wanted my children to meet my needs ("you're gonna be great at track"), and wanted to solve problems for them ("you should have punched him back!"). We survived it, but not without pain.

I don't wish this kind of pain on anybody, or their families.

2
A DIFFERENT APPROACH TO MANAGEMENT

ANYONE WHO HAS started a company knows that it's critical for the founders to be aligned when it comes to priorities and values. When Roberto and I talked about merging our companies, he said, "I want to build a company that works for everyone." That simple notion—that everyone should enjoy their work and share in the wealth—was at the foundation of the company. We were also in lockstep on a long list of things we didn't want at Nearsoft—we didn't want to be bosses, we didn't want "employees," we didn't want titles, we didn't want to hide information about the company, and so on.

It all took time to evolve, learning many lessons along the way. But, strange as it sounds, it took a crisis to convince us that we were on our way.

Near-Death Experience

The Nearsoft story almost came to an end after barely getting off the ground. In hindsight, this near-death experience was the best thing to happen to us because it showed us that we could manage the company without bosses.

In 2009 the financial crisis hit us.[11] Several of our clients folded, some reduced the size of their teams, and others stopped spending on anything but the bare necessities.

We tried all kinds of things, but by mid-year it was pretty clear that we had to roll back our expenses or else. Ironically, Roberto and I had just started to pay ourselves a steady salary and Nearsoft had moved into new offices, with room to grow.

Here to Stay

We were faced with the prospect of laying people off unless everyone tightened their belts a couple of notches. The "reasonable" thing to do would have been for Roberto and I to draw a list of people to lay off and that would have been it. I don't think people would have questioned it back then. They would not be surprised that we, as owners, did this. In fact, they might have excused it ("they did their best... they had to do it...").

But we would have known that it wasn't "our best." I know that I would have felt terrible and lost sleep over it for a long time; I suspect it would have been just as bad for Roberto. Instead, we did the most "democratic" thing we could think of at the time: we put it to a vote. (That ended up being the only time we've voted on anything, having since realized that voting is a pretty ham-fisted way of making decisions.)

After telling people what was happening and sharing the details of where we were financially, we suggested that we all take a 10% cut in salary. That would allow us to keep going through the end of the year when, we hoped, things would change for the better.

We voted, and… the proposal was rejected.

We were disappointed, to say the least. We were strongly tempted to just do it all ourselves at that point, but we didn't. The Force[12] held strong and we tried again.

After we cooled off, we could see that taking a pay cut didn't make sense to most people. For one, we had not yet formalized a stock option plan, so nobody else even had a financial stake in the company. Sure, they would be preserving their jobs, but they all could get new jobs easily.

They would be leaving behind a work space where we treated each other as adults and instead go back to having to "pretty please" the boss for everything. But at that point, co-management at Nearsoft was new and untested. Maybe the naysayers were right and it would eventually fade away.

Finally, there was the very real likelihood that come the end of the year, we might have to close down the company anyway. And in the meantime, the nail-biting would be intense.

So, we tried a different approach.

All of us talked and decided to form a committee to decide who was in and who was out. Several people were voted onto this committee. Roberto and I deliberately stayed out of this process. After a couple of days, the committee was done and we did as they had decided. It was painful, but to my surprise, it was not demoralizing.

Being part of the process, however imperfect, meant that there were no surprises. There was no hand-wringing over whether or not it was fair. There was no second-guessing why certain people had been let go and not others. The folks who sat on the committee could, and did, explain their choices, one peer to another.

It had been scary and messy, but it also made it clear that our fledgling co-management at Nearsoft was here to stay. If we could deal with this very difficult decision as a team, then we could manage the company as a team. We had to figure out how to do it, but that, we hoped, would be the fun part.

Inspired by a Maverick

About a year after the founding of Nearsoft, one of the authors, Adrian Perez, discovered a book called Maverick[13] and he insisted that I read it. About a third into the book, I excitedly badgered Roberto to read it. And he did—in one sitting.

Maverick is a book about a Brazilian manufacturer which Ricardo Semler, its author, inherited from his father. He tried to manage things his dad's way, but that didn't go well. After suffering a nervous breakdown, Semler decided to remake the company, to make it truly people centric in a non-patriarchal way. This meant things like letting people decide their own hours of operation, instituting profit-sharing, having workers sit on Board meetings, and opening the books and training people to make sense of them.

It was a head-exploding moment for us. Somebody had done it before. It showed us a path. And it helped put co-management at Nearsoft on a firmer footing. Other early books that have been very influential in our journey were Tribal Leadership,[14] PEAK,[15] and The Dream Manager.[16]

From the very start, we wanted to create a place where people could be themselves, enjoy each other, and contribute in unexpected, innovative ways. From personal experience, I knew that traditional management was painful and dehumanizing for all involved, bosses and workers alike—Roberto and I didn't want any of that. Semler's Maverick helped us see that we were not crazy or naïve for wanting something different. Maverick sketched out tools that we could use. And it showed us that we could shape a different future for all of us at Nearsoft.

Most of all, it made it clear that co-management wasn't just the absence of titles, corner offices, and managers. It required the development of a whole new organizational structure and practices.

It sounded like a lot of work, and it has been. And it's been worth it every step of the way. It allowed Nearsoft to thrive, not just survive. We made a bunch of mistakes along the way, but we also learned from them.

We also got some very big things right, including our approach to distributed decision making, which we call Leadership Teams, and the way we distribute dividends.

Leadership Teams

Leadership Teams are a light-weight mechanism for decentralized decision making. They are a key practice at Nearsoft.

"Leadership" is somewhat confusing for new people and they assume that it has to do with Roberto and me. They don't immediately recognize that *they* are the leaders and *they* are the ones who bring people together in a Leadership Team, at any time, for any purpose.

The only "rule" is that the Team be transparent and publish their minutes and conclusions. People who are going to be impacted by the decision must be involved in shaping it. There is no requirement to have one person speak at a time, or hold a symbolic stick, or any other procedure like that, although a Leadership Team may use these and other practices, if appropriate.

What "involved" means depends on the situation, but in general it includes "no surprises." It may include a consultation step, a bit reminiscent of the Advice Process, a term coined by Dennis Bakke at AES Corp to refer to the concept of "empowering team members who identify a problem or opportunity to take the initiative to address the situation." In our case, we don't empower anybody—we all come with all the power we need. And since there are no bosses at Nearsoft, there's no requirement to "ask your boss" as there is with Bakke's Advice Process[17], simply bounce it off somebody who knows about it more than you do.

Leadership Teams tackle all types of decisions at Nearsoft and have been remarkably effective in terms of engaging people in the process, resulting in better decisions. Nothing about us without us.[18]

Earned Dividends

From the very start, we shared the company's Dividends at Nearsoft. Roberto developed a distribution formula which worked for us for a while. Roberto's formula got very sophisticated, so much so that most people didn't understand it. But we all trusted Roberto and we knew that it must be fair. As we kept growing, the formula got even more inscrutable and in 2014, a small group of people decided to change it. They formed a Leadership Team and went about revising the Earned Dividends formula.

A former Nearsoftian, Luis Galaz, brought together a Leadership Team and they went to work. They tried out different ideas and consulted with lots of people and in general they treated the decision as what leadership author and consultant David Marquet calls a below-the-waterline decision, a decision critical to the health of the company.[19]

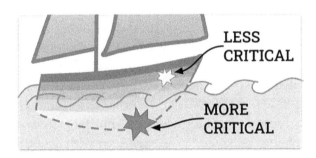

When they finally came out with a new formula, it was very simple: in the future, the end-of-year distribution would be calculated by dividing the total Earned Dividends by the number of Nearsoftians. That was it. Everyone would get an equal part of it. And that meant everybody, from the people responsible for cleaning and our van driver to Roberto and me.

Not everybody thought it was a good idea. "It ignores my contribution!" "What about all the years I spent going to school?" There were lots of questions, but no significant push back. There was consent as Sociocracy practitioners would call it, so we decided to try it for a couple of years. "If it doesn't work, you can form another Leadership Team that incorporates whatever we learned from the experience."

Roberto and I were among the people who didn't quite like it and I was fully expecting that it would not last. Then, one day in the Hermosillo kitchen, I heard a new Nearsoftian call it "too simplistic!" The answer, from another Nearsoftian, was powerful: "Look, we did as well as we did because of everybody, right? Trying to split hairs about specific contributions would be counter-productive, don't you think? And who would be the judge of that?" That made sense to me. As much as anything else, this "formula" was easy to understand and there is no wizard behind the curtain deciding how to split the wealth we all worked for. You could *trust it* to be fair.

And, in the words of Nobel Prize winner Elinor Ostrom, "Right at the center of trying to understand how people solve dilemmas is the challenge of their developing trust in one another."[20]Trust removes many of the worries that otherwise can sap people's energy. A more complicated formula may be technically more complete, but it's not necessarily better. "It is trying to hide something." On the other hand, an easy-to-understand formula can be trusted and not have to worry that they are being suckered. "We ended up with $1,000 in the till and there are 10 of us, so we each get $100."

It's worth noting that an equitable distribution is the goal, not equality. We'll say more about this in the second part of this book.

Totally Nuts

When we tell people outside the company about our wealth sharing, they think we are nuts. Nearsoft had no outside investors or shareholders, so all profits are distributed as Earned Dividends among all Nearsoftians. As a friend told me, this practice was "naïve and totally nuts and it will never work at any other business."

How to Not Motivate People

It's important to note that at Nearsoft, we don't use Earned Dividends as a form of motivation. That comes from inside each of us. Outside of work people readily self-direct and do what they have to do to meet their commitments.

Profit Sharing programs, as they are popularly known, usually try to reward things like,

- Extraordinary individual accomplishments
- Individual Experience
- Individual Academic degrees and other accreditations
- Individual contributions to the company's financial performance
- Management prerogative

Straight from Theory X,[21]the presumption is that all it takes is cash to motivate all those "indolent and irresponsible" people. But a once-a-year bump in income does nothing to promote any changes the following year. "A satisfied need (for money) no longer motivates."[22]Once they get their annual bonus, people go back to doing what's expected of them. As a means of, "motivating them, controlling their actions, modifying their behavior to fit the needs of the organization,"[23] the annual bonus doesn't work.

Freeloading

A question that comes up regularly, is about freeloading. How do you prevent people from taking advantage of it all? The short answer is that freeloading does not happen in co-managed companies like Nearsoft.

Freeloading happens in the FIAT context because 1) freeloading is considered a sin or a disease, 2) the boss has to catch the freeloader in the act, because 3) the freeloader's co-workers don't care to report it when they see it.

At Nearsoft, we have not experienced freeloading as such. In the few cases where people were not delivering on what they've promised, or repeatedly gave the-dog-ate-my-homework kind of excuses, there was something else going on that led to that behavior. It was not laziness or evil intent or a case of stealing from thy neighbor. Freeloading is usually a symptom, not the disease.

In one case it turned out that the "freeloader" was so used to being told what to do that when nobody said anything, he just didn't do anything. This happened in the very early days of Nearsoft. In all other cases, it turned out to be a side-effect of depression, or something happening at home or something along those lines. In one case it was about self-medicating that led to addiction and then got out of hand.

In each case, Nearsoftians dealt with it according to its circumstances. In one case, we had to let one person go; in other cases, Nearsoftians managed to get people the help they needed to deal with their personal situations. In the addiction case, Nearsoftians got his family involved, they got him back to health, and he continues to be a healthy Nearsoftian to this day.

3
GOOD NEWS!

NEARSOFT WAS ACQUIRED in 2017. Roberto and I hadn't planned on selling Nearsoft, but in 2015, the economic and political picture in the US and Mexico started to look unstable and we were getting a bit nervous. In any case, even though we were not looking for a buyer, a buyer found us.

It sounds weird now, even to me, but at the time, we didn't even think of involving anybody else in the decision. We just didn't think of it at the time. In fact, the concept of co-ownership didn't come into focus for me until *after* the acquisition.

It's Official

Nearsoft had been successfully acquired! The majority of Nearsoftians owned a piece of the company and benefited financially from the sale. As Roberto had said, the effort had worked "for everyone."

To top it off, the new owners recognized the value of the co-managed culture that had developed at Nearsoft. They liked our level of engagement and appreciated "the energy" they sensed at Nearsoft.

It was time to celebrate.

We knew that we would have to explain what it meant to each and every one of us. Being a shareholder had not meant much to most Nearsoftians up to this point. Holding a piece of paper that said that "you own ye many shares" had very little context in Mexico, even in the technology sector.

We knew that adults don't like surprises and people would be concerned, but this one was unavoidable. At one point during these talks we signed a Non-disclosure Agreement and had to keep the whole process under wraps. And now that it was done the questions gushed out: How is this going to impact me? Am I going to lose my job? Will it change Nearsoft's culture?

The easiest thing to explain was what it meant financially. Most Nearsoftians owned a piece of the company and they would benefit directly from the acquisition. Even the newbies benefited because those of us who had shares were taken off the Earned Dividend pool and the newbies got the whole pool for themselves (*i.e.*, the numerator stayed the same while the denominator got a lot smaller).

Roberto had warned me that people were going to be very surprised, even shocked. I nodded my head in agreement then, but it didn't quite sink in. After more than 30 years in technology in Silicon Valley, "exits" were old hat for me. Not so for the other Nearsoftians. As the actual checks started to come in, people were still a bit incredulous. "Can I take my kids to Disneyland? Can I buy a house?"

The concerns that came up later took longer to deal with.

Great, But…

The most common questions were about the future of Nearsoft and our distinct culture. Nearsoftians valued it, dearly, and the acquisition could be a threat to it. Would we get managers now? Would the new owners change how we do things?

As fear crept up on people, all kinds of rumors arose about what might be coming. Luckily, people were used to speaking up, even about issues like this. For us, that's one of the many values of co-management: learning to be responsible for your concerns, voicing them, and resolving them collaboratively. A rumor would come up, somebody would bring it out in the open, and the answers would be discussed, digested, and disseminated throughout Nearsoft. After about a month or so, things settled down.

A Lot Left to Be Done

The acquisition was more evidence that co-management not only worked, but it worked better than FIAT management. The money that would have gone to bosses, we spent it on ourselves instead and still managed to generate a very healthy profit margin.

We hold two Team Building Weeks every year where all Nearsoftians come to work together in one place. Clients join us, too.

In Spring, we usually go to a nice place, like Cancún, or a place of historical significance, like Querétaro. New friendships, and even romances, are started. The Winter Team Building Week is capped off with a grand end-of-year party. We can afford to do things like this because we don't waste money on bosses and the perception of control.

By the way, these Team Building events weren't always a hit, but they are an example of what happens when the organizers and the participants are the same people. The feedback we got from the first couple of events was pretty negative. "Why do I have to waste time playing these stupid games." "The speaker didn't know anything about us." "We paid this guy (the invited speaker) for that bullshit?" But because the organizers were also participants, they kept making them more useful over time by simply doing less of what sucked and more of what worked.

People have blossomed into the leaders they didn't think they could be. Introverts with quiet voices have led the creation of events of all sizes, like NearsoftCon, a full-blown event with external speakers and all the rest of it. We've seen people grow in ways that would have been impossible in the shadow of a FIAT hierarchy. I like to think that their growth has benefited their families and communities, too.

Regardless of all the good stuff, there's a lot more to be done, particularly, in the area of ownership. Self-management is becoming more popular and all, but it is not enough.

Co-Management Is Not Enough

My own questions started to bubble up a couple of years after the acquisition. I felt good about it and the team we had joined, that was not the issue. We had moved to a bigger stage, from a regional player to a global one. It also gave us a chance to learn and that was good.

Regardless, I had the sense that there was other work left to be done. Yes, we had all benefited financially, but most of us had not learned to be owners, at least not fully, even though we had haphazardly taken a step in that direction (*e.g.*, changing the Earned Dividends scheme which normally is an owner's prerogative). But there was so much more that we hadn't explored. Take capital allocation.

Each year, Roberto and I decided how much of our profits to use as capital for the following year and how much to leave in the Dividend pool. It just never occurred to us to include others in this decision. If we had thought of it, we would probably have dismissed the idea right off. "They don't understand Nearsoft's financial situation, so why put this on them?"

We decided how to divide the pie and the size of the employee pool. We chose how to allocate the shares in that pool and decided how many shares each cohort would get. All very reasonable and fair. We were the owners, so we made the call. But in doing so, what issues were we blind to? What opportunities had we missed? These and similar questions were bouncing around in my head.

After a while it all started to come together for me: co-management was not enough! We needed a model of ownership that went beyond financial benefits. A system that would survive us, the Enlightened Monarchs. A model that formally decentralized ownership distribution, capital allocation, and all other aspects of being an owner. And we needed to figure out how to get everybody involved in dealing with these issues.

4
THE FIAT
APOCALYPSE

Unhappy at Work

You've probably seen the claim that "people are unhappy at work." It's all over the Web in blogs, videos, surveys, and academic papers. It is very dramatic, makes good headlines, and it is also very true.

Gallup probably is the premier source of this kind of data. According to one of their reports, "The global aggregate from Gallup data collected in 2014, 2015 and 2016 across 155 countries indicates that just 15% of employees worldwide are engaged in their job. Two-thirds are not engaged and 18% are actively disengaged."[24] To be clear, "actively disengaged" means that more than unhappy, these people are numb.

You may not be all that unhappy, not in general. At least, not all the time. You like the people you work with; most of them, in any case. And the work itself is not quite bad. It's just that things could be better.

I've been extremely lucky. I really enjoy what I do and the people I do it with. At our company we make up its rules and policies and when they no longer work, we change them. Some, like Paul Buchheit[25] are even luckier. He is the creator of Gmail and has worked at Sun Microsystems and Facebook and ended up a very wealthy person. In his words,

> "I don't have to work. I choose to work. And I believe everyone deserves the same freedom I have. If done right, it's also economically superior, meaning we will all have more wealth. We often talk about how brilliant or visionary Steve Jobs was, but there are probably millions of people just as brilliant as he was. The difference is they likely didn't grow up with great parents, amazing teachers, and an environment where innovation was the norm. Also they didn't live down the street from Steve Wozniak.

> "Economically, we don't need more jobs. We need more Steve Jobs.

> "When we set everyone free, we enable the outliers everywhere. The result will be an unprecedented boom in human creativity and ingenuity."

Why aren't we all this "lucky?" Why can't we extend this type of "luck" to more people, like everybody involved in creating and growing a company, not just the founders and the investors?

If we get even close to broadening this "luck," more people would be more engaged and fully alive. Or as economist Umai Haque put it we'd be "rich with relationships, ideas, emotion, health and vigor, recognition and contribution, passion and fulfillment, and great accomplishment and enduring achievement."[26]I have a hunch that our economy would also grow healthier, more just, and financially stronger.

The Other Huge Problem

The other huge problem is Capitalism, as currently practiced.

Once upon a time, to me, Capitalism was the opposite of Communism. Communism was Fidel Castro's dictatorship in Cuba, where I was born and raised, and Capitalism was the US Declaration of Independence and Benjamin Franklin. At the age of 14, my family got me out to Spain which, at the time, was also a dictatorship. It was less dysfunctional than Cuba's, but it was a dictatorship nevertheless. It started to look like things were not as simple as I had once thought.

These days I recognize that what we call Capitalism is severely broken and hurts the overwhelming majority of us. It even hurts those who benefit most from it financially, although they don't talk about it with the exception of Warren Buffet and precious few others, such as billionaire Ray Dalio,[27]who in 2019 stated, "Capitalism basically is not working for the majority of people."

I am not aching for a revolution. Revolutions just bring in a different set of bosses without changing the structure itself for the better. More generally, we are not thinking of government as the solution. Rather than relying on policies and taxes to fix it, people can transform the system from the ground up and from the inside out. This can happen without doing away with the good aspects of capital. If we transform ownership, then Capitalism will change along with it. In the RADICAL paradigm, ownership remains private but it is much broader and dynamic than today.

FIAT Businesses

The big obstacle to this transformation is our current concept of ownership. "This is my business, not yours." This assumption is invisible, taken for granted.

We don't even have an umbrella term for all the forms of private ownership. We have sole ownerships, partnerships, and various forms of corporations. I could not find a term for all of them as a class, so we made one up: we call these FIAT businesses. Run as dictatorships and owned like feudal estates.

At the top of the hierarchy is an oligarchy, the Board of Directors, and below them are their proxy bosses, the Executives. Below them are lesser bosses, and ever lesser bosses below them. At the very bottom is everybody else. Altogether they make up what we call a FIAT hierarchy. This hierarchy is all about executing the will of the FIAT owners. These owners control all the wealth the business creates. They are fiduciarily responsible to act in the interest of shareholders, which has come to mean that they have to make sure the business is profitable. Everything else is secondary, at best. "What's good for the business is good for the workers."[28]

We might have gotten rid of the divine right of kings and queens in the political realm, but we didn't do anything about the divine right of capital. We left the corporate aristocracy, the heirs of the landowners and enslaver class, in control of the wealth and who partakes of it.

Behind the front door of every FIAT business, the owners still rule as kings and queens.

Twenty-First Century Feudalism

Most businesses today are run like feudal estates. Only the owners are entitled to make decisions, regardless of the impact to employees. Only they have the authority to decide on matters of ownership. Who gets how many shares? How much in retained earnings? How much to keep for themselves? How much to distribute as bonuses?

Employees don't get to participate in making any of these decisions. And the same goes for common shareholders who don't have a say in any of this, either.

5
READY FOR WAR

War Machines

Businesses are envisioned as war machines. Today's businesses are rife with war terms and metaphors. Battle-tested strategy, rally the troops, capture a market, dominate a segment. We've ended up with a militarized economy that takes a toll on everybody's well-being.

Enough!

We need to step away from this "economy that is dependent on perpetual war"[30] before it obliterates us. We need a different enough paradigm that is sustainable in the long-term. We need an economy that won't crush us under its weight. Or as Mark Carney, governor of the Bank of England said in 2020, we need "… a fit planet for our grandchildren to live on."[31] Businesses don't have to be ready for war at all times.

Even if they were in a battle with live bullets, they don't need to be at war at all times.

Pirates knew that.

Pirates and Democracy

In pirate ships of yore "Captains retained absolute authority in times of battle."[32]The rest of the time, the navigator could argue with the Captain all day long, and sailors could vote for a destination other than the one favored by the Captain. But during battle, do as the Captain says (or else). This was one of the things spelled out in a constitution-like document that the real pirates of the Caribbean operated by.

These constitutions even spelled out how much of the loot each sailor would get. Generally, sailors would get one unit of the loot, the Quartermaster one and half, and the Captain two units. When it's all said and done, pirates were a pretty RADICAL bunch.

CEOs are often called "Captain of the ship." This is problematic in many ways, not the least of which is that this means FIAT businesses are engaged in a perpetual war. Through that looking glass, all they see is enemies. The cost of employees, customer support, supplier pricing: they are all enemies clawing away at my loot… er… profits. We talk with pride about *capturing* customers and locking them in. *Crushing* the competition. Putting golden *handcuffs* on "the best" employees. *Locking them up* with sign-on bonuses (that they'd have to pay back if they leave).

This is pathological, at best. It's not surprising that people feel tense, bosses and employees alike. If, as a boss, you view yourself as a battle Captain, then you'll expect people to jump overboard at your say so, of course. As a boss, the frustration you feel when people don't immediately do as you say arises from that expectation. I've felt this frustration myself and it is still with me, albeit more subdued, even after many years of being part of this grand experiment called Nearsoft.

As an employee you are always in battle mode, too. You get good at following the Captain's command, or at least pretending to do so. Don't speak up, don't argue, just say ay, ay, sir (and be ready to blame it on somebody else if it doesn't work).

People have internalized this constant state of battle; the boss has embraced the Captain persona and employees have learned to salute without a second thought. No wonder people feel stressed at work: they spend their days in a war zone.

A Peacetime Company

We wondered why there hasn't been a move to "stand down" over time, a move away from the perpetual war position. After a horrific conflagration like WWII, why didn't we get wise to the need for a different approach? Particularly, given the post-WWII economic expansion[33] and the sustained period of growth and prosperity that followed, why didn't we adopt more of a peacetime model for our businesses and our economy?

Ernst Bader got an inkling of this war stance and wanted to move his company away from it. Bader had founded the Scott Bader company in 1921. In 1951, right after WWII, Bader and his family turned 90% of their shares to a Trust and all the company's dividends to its *members* (*i.e.*, that's what he called them to differentiate them from *employees*). He wanted to promote "an alternative to a war-based capitalist economy."[34]

A few years later W L Gore and Associates took the peacetime path from the start. In 1958, Bill and Genevieve Gore founded their company in their basement.[35] From the start, the company didn't have bosses or assigned teams. They were aware of the scaling issue built into traditional hierarchies and of how bureaucracy takes over as companies get bigger. As author Bernard Schroeder writes, "… Bill Gore felt that when a unit of workers got big enough, it actually began to fall apart. Gore understood that workers in a 150-person unit could all know one another and share a commitment to group goals and values and that any growth beyond that would change those dynamics."[36] The 150-person number is now known as the Dunbar number, but Bill Gore came to it by trial and error.[37]

In the long run, it has worked out really well for them. "Gore has grown revenues to nearly $3 billion and consistently turned a profit since its founding in 1958. It has approximately 9000 employees at 30 locations worldwide."[38] As of this writing, the company generates $3.7 billion in annual revenues and over 10,500 associates worldwide who are also co-owners of the company.

W L Gore & Associates has accomplished this without an all-powerful battle Captain at the helm. It is the closest example of a co-managed and co-owned company that we know of and it is fantastically successful and inspirational.

6
THE OWNERSHIP PUZZLE

A Society of Kings

In 1776, the US became the first tangible instantiation of
Enlightenment ideals. We the people could govern ourselves
better than King George III could. He was no longer the
owner of everything and citizens would be the owners instead.
Decentralized property was the key to our liberty. But this
new form of government, a republican democracy, was going
to be run by property owners, freeholders, and men of leisure,
people who had "time given to study and becoming enlightened about universal truths and appropriate governmental
policies."[39]

Unfortunately, this narrowed considerably who was a citizen, with the right to vote and to own property. By design, it

excluded women, Native Americans, and most definitely the enslaved[40] who were the "property" that made up a significant part of the wealth of said citizens. It also excluded from voting anybody who had to labor for a living, namely poor whites. Laborers were financially dependent on the owner class and were not considered free enough to vote.

The new system decentralized ownership but in a very limited way. Nevertheless, it enshrined private property as the basis of liberty: the power that previously had been reserved for King George III was now in the hands of a society of kings—owners of land, owners of people.

1792 Profit-Sharing

The founders did know about co-ownership and were aware of its virtues. As Dr Joseph Blasi points out in *A Founding Father Profit Sharing Fix for Inequality*,

"On February 16, 1792, Washington signed into law a bill from the U.S. Congress that cut taxes for ship owners and sailors in the American cod fishery, in an effort to revive the failing industry. However, the tax cut was conditioned on a broad-based profit-sharing arrangement between shipowners and the crews—a centuries-long custom of sharing the profits made from every catch. The legislation was supported by two politicians who typically agreed on very little: Secretary of the Treasury Alexander Hamilton and Secretary of State Thomas Jefferson... ships with profit-sharing were more productive than those with fixed wages."[41]

In any case, it would be unfair and more than a little arrogant to rain on the founders' parade from today's perspective. What they did was very revolutionary at the time. The Declaration of Independence is aspirationally brilliant for its time. The economic system that emerged has brought us a lot of material good, but it has also caused a lot of misery. And as it is, the system is fast approaching an ugly dead end, but we must not submit to this fate.

We will find ways to preserve our common good, our commonwealth. Management author and venerated guru, Peter Drucker believed that businesses could be a force for good, but he assumed that only bosses could do it: "If the managers of our major institutions, and especially of business, do not take responsibility for the common good, no one else can or will."[42] Well, nearly 50 years have passed since Drucker wrote this and the bosses have not taken "responsibility for the common good." Wish as we will, bosses will not be the agents of benevolent change that Drucker imagined.

Although he was wrong about the bosses, Drucker was right in implying that businesses could be effective agents of change. As Kim Jordan, co-founder of New Belgium Brewing, put it, "Business is a powerful tool in making the kind of world that we want to live in."[43]

Everything that developed at New Belgium over the years was RADICAL: the use of Open Book Management, an ESOP[44] (Employee Stock Ownership Plan) through which its workers eventually owned 100%[45] of the company, and the involvement of everybody in planning and managing the company. Everybody at New Belgium felt like owners because they were the real owners, not symbolic owners. One of them exclaimed that he could deal with the complex paperwork and negotiations of buying a house, "because I'm an owner in New Belgium, and there's Open-Book Management, then I'm able to do this $500,000 transaction. A warehouse worker, a forklift driver is doing this."[46]

Karl Marx

Karl Marx tried his hand at the ownership issue. Unfortunately, his formulation assumed the same FIAT hierarchy paradigm: there's gotta be a boss, so the proletariat shall be the boss. Instead of having all the wealth concentrated in the hands of oligarchs, put it in the hands of the proletariat, the people who produced the wealth in the first place.

Inspired by Marx, the Bolsheviks rallied behind Lenin to instantiate this ideal in 1917.[47] Unfortunately, since Marx hadn't really figured out how to implement the proletariat-as-boss concept, it fell to the Bolshevik dictatorship to play the role of the all-powerful, universal boss. On behalf of the proletariat, of course.

Spoiler alert: it didn't work well for anybody, particularly the proletariat.

Henry George

In 1879 Henry George,[48] an American economist, published *Progress and Poverty*.[49] The book became really popular and by the 1890s it was second only to the Christian Bible in the number of copies sold in the US. It also caught on throughout the world and even inspired San Yat-sen, "one of the greatest leaders of modern China."[50]

According to George, rent from land should accrue to society, not to landowners. A vacant lot in a growing neighborhood would go up in value by virtue of the improvements around it. As others build houses, businesses, and parks nearby, the value of the vacant lot goes up.

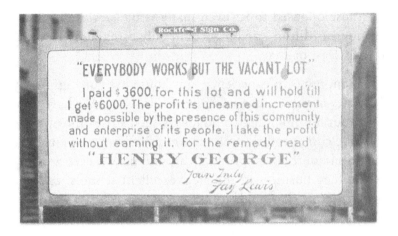

EVERYBODY WORKS BUT THE VACANT LOT" – I paid $3600 for this lot and will hold 'till I get $6000. The profit is unearned increment made possible by the presence of this community and enterprise of its people. I take the profit without earning it. For the remedy read "HENRY GEORGE

— Yours Truly, Fay Lewis.[51]

It follows then that the new, higher rent should go to the community who raised the value of the land, not the landowner who did nothing for it. George noted that "nothing that is freely supplied by nature can be properly classed as capital."[52]

Landowners would keep the rights to profit for any improvements, but not the rent for the land itself. People could farm it or build houses on it and the results of their work and investment would still belong to them. But the rent from the land itself belongs to society. As professor Dr Francis Peddle put it, "The return to labour and capital is for George inalienable relative to the individual, while the return to land (nature) ought to be appropriated by society."[53]

George's proposal featured a land tax as a way for society to recover the rent that the landowner was not entitled to. As much as anything else, this made the proposal an easy target for those opposed to it. Even many years later, well-known economist Milton Friedman could only bring himself to call it, "the least bad tax."[54]

From my own experience, our house has gone up nearly 10 times in value since we bought it in 1984. We have kept it up, but nothing that would justify such a rise. The upsurge in value comes mostly from community improvements: the beautiful houses that sprung up around us, the ever-growing technology business in the area, excellent schools, and the infrastructure that holds it together.

Monopoly

I first heard about George in the context of the game of Monopoly. The game was invented by Elizabeth Phillips (neé Magie)[55] and originally had two sets of rules.[56] In the "monopolist" version, called The Landlord's Game, players would buy property and charge rent to other players; a player wins when all others go broke. Those are the rules that survive as today's Monopoly game.

The anti-monopolist version, later called Prosperity, showed how George's proposals would deal with the problems that traditional ownership of land created. In this version of the game, players would benefit through a single tax on land. With this tax the community would buy private services (*e.g.*, commuter train services) and make them free to all players. The land owners could keep the wealth created by their labor and capital investments, untaxed.

Broad Impact

Henry George and his single land tax idea inspired a multitude of people, including economist John Bates Clark, who observed that "profit-sharing makes the workman, in a sense, an employer; and full cooperation makes him both an employer and a capitalist."[57] It seems that Clark came very close to the concepts of co-ownership ("profit sharing... an employer") and co-management ("full cooperation... a capitalist") from the work of Henry George.

His words had an indelible effect on George Bernard Shaw, "I went one night, quite casually, into a hall in London, and I heard a man deliver a speech which changed the whole current of my life. That man was an American, Henry George."[58]

Hellen Keller waxed poetic about his philosophy, "I know I shall find in Henry George's philosophy a rare beauty and power of inspiration and a splendid faith in the essential nobility of human nature."[59]

Even Albert Einstein was enthusiastic about it, "Men like Henry George are rare unfortunately. One cannot imagine a more beautiful combination of intellectual keenness, artistic form, and fervent love of justice. Every line is written as if for our generation."[60]

George's proposal is said to also have influenced many of the New Deal initiatives.[61]

However, in spite of all the enthusiasm it generated, replacing all taxes with a single land tax never came to pass. His ideas were "adopted to some degree in Australia, Hong Kong, Singapore, South Africa, South Korea, and Taiwan..."[62] More recently the town of Altoona, Pennsylvania, temporarily implemented it, "... phasing in the tax in 2002, relying on it entirely for tax revenue from 2011, and ending it 2017."[63]

Fear, Uncertainty, and Doubt

Reading George's master opus raised a question: it was such a straightforward idea and backed by many luminaries and powerful people. Why didn't it stick?

One possible reason is that it must have been fairly easy to scare landowners into opposition. For example, what would the Roman Catholic church be without the rent from its extensive land holdings? Ditto for other landholding organizations.

Would the same thing happen to co-ownership? It might get people excited initially, but would it take hold and make a practical difference in the world?

The big difference is that co-ownership does not require messing around with taxes nor getting governments into the business of collecting rent. Rather, co-ownership seeks to decentralize the ownership of companies, and this can be done by regular people without government involvement. Undoubtedly, there will be significant opposition to co-ownership, but it won't be easily brushed off as yet another government mandate.

Louis O Kelso

Our suspicion is that the key reason why George's proposal and others like it have not taken root is because they ignored private businesses. Or maybe they didn't ignore businesses but thought of them as a lost cause. Either way, it seems that the biggest miscalculation has been to go straight to government solutions, leaping over businesses.

Henry George was definitely an original thinker, a brilliant observer, and thought well outside the box. He worried and wrote about our lopsided wealth distribution and saw the problem clearly. But when it came to implementation, George, like many others, jumped to the tools of government: regulations, taxes, redistribution. He and many other writers and reformers assumed that businesses could only be changed by coercion, and only the government, the biggest boss of all, could bring enough force to bear to make it happen. Only the government could save the little people from abusive, mean business owners.

The inventor and pioneer of what became known as the Employee Stock Ownership Plans (ESOP), Louis O Kelso, didn't ignore businesses. His big contribution was to figure out how to entice the not-so-enlightened bosses to help workers partake in the wealth created by the companies they worked for.

He was keenly aware that poverty was a human invention, but rather than propping up the poor with handouts, his aim was to eliminate poverty altogether or at least reduce it in a major way. Unfortunately, he, too, ended up getting involved with government.

Kelso was on the right track when he wrote, "What needs to be adjusted is the opportunity to produce, not the redistribution of income after it's produced."[64] His idea was to make the workers owners of the businesses they worked for. If businesses are money-making machines, then set it up so that the workers end up as owners of these machines and of the wealth they generate. However, he made the same mistake that earlier reformers made—he, too, assumed that there had to be a boss and probably didn't think of eliminating the FIAT hierarchy; in any case, that was not part of his scheme. This made the workers symbolic owners only, financial beneficiaries but not real owners. But ownership is a lot more than financial benefits and impacts people's lives beyond their work.[65] More important than the monetary gains, owners decide many things that affect employees most often without them knowing it. It is something that most of us never learn about. A home is a passive asset, at best, but home ownership is not the same as being the owner of a productive asset, one that actively generates wealth, like a business.

PART TWO
AN ALTERNATIVE
TO OUR BROKEN
SYSTEM

9
THE RADICAL PARADIGM

OUR DEEPEST PROBLEMS are the inescapable side-effects of the FIAT system we live in, a system based on domination: our collapsing climate, the gaping wealth gap, discrimation against people of color, the exploitation of women. We need a generative way of relating to one another, a different paradigm. As we see it, companies are the place to start, they are the appropriate incubators for what comes next.

Nature follows a simple path to create big beautiful things out of unpretentious, small ones. From tiny seed to mighty oak tree. We don't think that a long list of principles or color scales or a 17 page constitution are necessary to make a fundamental change. Eventually, these can become dogma and get in the way.

With that in mind, we came up with what we think are the most basic foundations to support our coming together to share work and wealth.

A Three Legged Stool

Every company is different because the people who embody it are different, so every company must find its own way. Having said that, we do have some opinions as to what fundamentally makes a RADICAL company different from a FIAT business.

Here's how we see the foundations of a RADICAL company,

Principles	Meaning and Belonging
Commitments	Transparency and Decentralization
Practices	Alignment and Experimentation

Other principles and practices can be layered on top of them, but for a RADICAL company these principles, commitments, and practices are essential, otherwise it is just a FIAT business with ain't-we-nice sprinkled on top.

We have lived in this FIAT world for a long time and the switch to RADICAL is not going to be instantaneous. As your company changes, you will learn and grow, but staying firm on these tenets will keep you on your path.

Unlike in a FIAT business, a hierarchy is not imposed in a co-managed company. The hierarchies that do emerge are dynamic, fluid, and shaped by what's needed, by the people involved, and a particular time. "An organism constantly changes. The cells develop, die and are replaced. It adapts to the current environment or goes away. ... The org chart is insufficient."[66]

For example, at W L Gore and Associates leaders are selected, not elected, by their followers. These are real leaders, not bosses-passing-as-leaders. If people are not happy with the leader or where their effort is heading, they simply leave and follow somebody else or start their own projects.[67]

According to Hamel et al, they do a similar thing at Haier: "New leaders are chosen competitively. Typically, three or four candidates will present their plans to the [Microenterprise] team. The discussions are intense, as team members press for details on how prospective leaders will get things back on track. Occasionally, a team rejects the entire slate of candidates and the search process goes to round two."[68]

At Valve they do something even more dramatic: desks are on wheels. When people want to leave a team, they roll their desks away. It sounds like it'd be fun to watch,

"Why does your desk have wheels? Think of those wheels as a symbolic reminder that you should always be considering where you could move yourself to be more valuable. But also think of those wheels as literal wheels, because that's what they are, and you'll be able to actually move your desk with them."[69]

At The Morning Star Company people come together around a task and disband when it's done.

In case you are wondering, the result is not chaos at Gore, Valve, Haier, or The Morning Star, all of which are very financially successful, thanks for asking. Gore has been doing this since 1958, The Morning Star Company since 1970, and Valve since 1997. According to Corporate Rebel co-founder Joost Minnaar, Haier has been at it since 2005.[70] So, it looks like in addition to being financially successful, these companies are resilient.

Principles: Meaning & Belonging (Jose Leal)

I started several businesses while I was in my late teens and rode the Internet wave all the way to the entrepreneurial dream: the successful exit. After our startup was acquired, my business partner Ron and I joined a top Canadian online media business.

I never thought of myself as a boss but found myself in that situation. I had what many people would consider a dream job—Vice President and General Manager. The business was in the middle of another significant round of growth, hiring executives and hundreds of staff. The corporate budget was nearing dot-com era levels and there was a push for another IPO, the second since I had joined the business. I recall saying, "I smell greed in the air." During the first IPO attempt, I was left to clean up mistakes made as things came to a crashing halt and everyone was thrown off the sinking ship. This time, I watched as those same mistakes were repeated and swore I wasn't going to do it again.

I hated not only the situation I was in but I hated that I had become everything I disliked about corporate types—a political, selfish, heartless hatchetman—at least outwardly. Inwardly, it was killing me and exacting a tremendous toll on my body and personal life. I was a complete mess. Just in time, I was able to negotiate my exit. By the end of that year, the executives and hundreds of staff were gone.

I quickly jumped back in the world of business and co-founded my fourth startup in the online marketing space. Initially, I was thrilled to be away from the corporate life and diving back into a new project. But as I look back on that time, I realize my heart was never in it. Every time things started to look promising, I lost interest. It dragged on for years. Eventually, both the startup and my marriage were coming to an end, and I was numb to it all.

While spending many months back in my birthplace of Portugal, helping to take care of my mother after her stroke, I dove deep into figuring out what had happened. I felt like I was finally starting to come out of the fog I had been in for years. The impact of those ten years had been worse than I had imagined and I couldn't understand how it had happened. How I had become so lost?

I've spent the last several years researching and studying what makes us human and what prompts us to certain actions and choices. Over and over I have found that meaning and belonging are at the center of it all, in a grand loop of inter-dependence, the human system that connects us and produces our culture. It is what helps people navigate their physical and social world.

At the center of them all are Meaning and Belonging. Meaning comes out of stories, and stories come out of the communities you belong to, where they make sense.

Meaning is what makes sense to each of us, what feels right. As entrepreneur, consultant, and author Chuck Blakeman says, "people want to make meaning, not just money."[71] We know when something, an action or act of kindness, is meaningful because it touches us.

I understand that we have to make money to eat, to pay the rent, to pay for school, to get to work. But what drives us is making sense of the world around us and discovering with others the many ways in which we can live our lives and apply our potential without hurting anyone. In a study published in Frontiers in Psychology, Hu and Hirsh found that "… participants reported minimum acceptable salaries that were 32% lower for personally meaningful jobs compared to jobs that were perceived as personally meaningless."[72]

Artists do their work because, to them, it is meaningful, even cathartic. They may or may not make a living at it, but they keep at it. All meaningful work is self-expression, is art.

People know that they belong in a group when they are aligned with it. People know that they belong when they feel safe and can count on other people's support because they understand each other's struggles. And it works in virtual communities, too, as in this tweet,

Alex "Warmly From 10 Feet Away" Anderson
@AlexAndersonMD

Thanks for being so incredibly nice and showing me grace when I share my weakness, failures, insecurities, etc here. Seriously thank you.

8:40 PM · May 9, 2020 · Twitter for iPhone   [73]

Author and consultant Nilofer Merchant[74] captured how meaning and belonging are two sides of the proverbial coin,

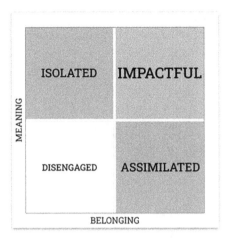

Commitments: Transparency & Decentralization (Matt Perez)

I spent most of my working life hiding things: information, actions, decisions, mistakes. I could make decisions that my subordinates couldn't. I am pretty sure that I made decisions that they could have made if only they had access to the right information. I certainly didn't want to repeat that at Nearsoft.

After reading Maverick, Roberto and I agreed to practice full disclosure and to decentralize decision-making. Decentralization was about opening things up so that everybody can make decisions, take responsibility, and be accountable to themselves and their peers. Transparency meant disclosing all the data known or generated by the company, but it is also about being vulnerable. Researcher-storyteller Brené Brown points out that, "in order for connections to happen, we have to allow ourselves to be seen—really seen."[75] This means, for example, asking for help when you need it, and accepting help even when you didn't know you needed it.

It is impossible to decentralize decision-making without making the necessary information transparent. And transparency without decentralization is simply frustrating, like seeing the candy behind that glass that you cannot reach.

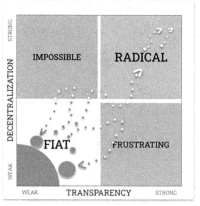

76

From my own experience at Nearsoft, you can never be 100% transparent or decentralized. Not because you don't want to, but because you can't see what you can't see. Even though we are very committed to both at Nearsoft, we still find things that are not as transparent or decentralized as we would like them to be. For example, Roberto and I decided on budgets by ourselves until somebody said something like, "These numbers are not going to work! Why didn't you ask me?" So we decentralized the budgeting process. In another instance, a group made a decision and somebody pointed out to them that it would increase overhead. "We didn't know... how do we find out what impacts overhead?"

If you don't commit to Transparency and Decentralization right out of the gate, none of the incremental, piece-meal approaches will make a lasting difference. Everybody in your company needs to develop the habit of asking themselves these questions whenever they write a document or come up with a new way of doing things. Am I making this information more transparent or less? Is this a more centralized or less centralized way of doing things? It will be painfully obvious to you if decisions that are important to you become more centralized or if somebody is purposely hiding information that's important for you and others to know. You'll feel it in your body when a particular task stops making sense to you but you have to keep doing it, or when you are forced to conform to the group norms and have no voice in the matter.

Don't worry if you are the only one who's noticed any of these threats. That's what makes you valuable to your group. Help them notice. Diversity is the collection of fears that renders them all powerless.

Practices: Alignment & Experimentation (Adrian Perez)

I have always been interested in what I would call the Third Way. It has seemed to me that often when dealing with a dichotomy, both sides are getting it wrong. You have two sides that are pushing and pulling over some territory and they get stuck in detente. This usually serves both sides, because it validates their survival. Whether it is traditional school or Montessori, Communism versus Capitalism, or any other such conflict, I look for the third way. In the case of schools, I found Sudbury Schools and Summersill. And for the case of how humans should organize their businesses, I have helped conceive the ideas in this book that we call RADICAL. The idea is to end the game that no longer serves us so we can create a whole new game. I enjoy shaking off the older system and removing the old impediments to human happiness, resilience, and personal power.

Having worked in software businesses in Silicon Valley, some growing and some collapsing, I have experienced the very informal and yet still very hierarchical, unimaginative, and stifling environments of corporate America.

We can do better.

It will take all of us, operating at our best to pull ourselves out of the nosedive that global civilization finds itself in. And it starts with explicit alignment. Alignment is what gets everybody to paddle in the same direction. You must make a habit of listening to the passionate voices in the group and embrace the vision that emerges.

For a FIAT business, its Impact and Purpose pretty much collapses to, "to generate wealth for the FIAT owner" and its Mission is whatever the boss wants, and where the boss wants it. For a RADICAL company, an explicit alignment does a better job of helping a group of people move in the same direction. With it in hand, adults can figure out how best to contribute. No boss needed, thank you.

Experimentation is the practice that gives shape to all other practices. Every proposal and every crazy idea must end up with something like, "should we try it?" Once asking this question becomes a habit, not doing it will feel odd, like something is missing. Experiment with any practice that you think will work, but experiment.

You'll get to experiment with all the things that are usually "required" at work, including, among many others, dress code, schedules, and location. For example, COVID-19 has forced the whole world to explore whether or not we need an office. Some people say that we'll never go back to offices, but others miss the social aspects of it. But even if we get physically together to work, does it have to be every day, every other day, or as needed? Does it have to be "at the office" or could it be elsewhere, anywhere?

Explore and discover what practices best support what works for you. Find your Third Way.

8
ALIGNMENT

The Scout Salute

When it is just you and a couple of friends on a walk, the direction is set quasi-randomly by one of you and the others follow as you all talk. No big deal. But creating a service or making a product is more complex than a walk in the park. We will need a robust, scalable way of deciding what to build and how to do it.

In order to create a RADICAL company, we will first need to be explicit about the company's *what for*, its *why*, and its *what*, *how*, and *when*. You might call them something different or you might lump some of these together. However you express them, they have to be explicit and completely open and accessible to everyone. The three-finger Scout Salute[77] is a good mnemonic for remembering the elements of an explicit alignment,

- Impact is our beacon, a clear point of light just over the horizon that guides us. This is what many call Vision but we wanted to put more emphasis on the *impact* that vision will have on the world.

- Dave Logan, lead author of *Tribal Leadership*, used to call it Noble Cause, but these days he prefers to call it Noble Passion. As he puts it, "… a noble cause gets you out of bed. A noble passion gets you out of bed early and keeps you up late into the night."[78]

- Purpose is the reason *why* we, as a company, are focused on this particular Impact. It doesn't have to be world shaking and it doesn't have to strum your heart's strings. An effective Purpose must clearly express *why* it is important for others to join us in this adventure.

- The Mission defines *what* we are going to do to move towards the Impact, *how* we are going to do it, and by *when*. In the case of Nearsoft, we have defined two five-year Missions, one in 2012 and another in 2017.[79] Everybody takes part in this: about 80 Nearsoftians in the first one, and around 300 participated in defining our latest Mission, as of this writing.

This is but one way to express alignment. The important thing is to make it explicit, simple, and intelligible to everybody in the team. I should be able to ask six people in the team, "What is our Purpose?" and get very similar answers, in their own words, and not six totally different answers.

To do their job, to be effective and present to everybody, our alignment choices have to be baked into everything we actually do, otherwise they are reduced to nice words collecting dust on a wall.

Values? OK, Values!

The other thing that we'd have to think about is Values.

This is not about the "Our Values" poster in the lobby. These are usually meaningless, something the boss came up with after reading an article on the subject. Normally, these get posted on a wall and that's that, or, worst, they get weaponized. "I hear that you are not much of a teamplayer, are you? Didn't you know that being a team player is one of our values?"

Values used to be very much in vogue as a tool of alignment and so in 2010, inspired by Tony Hsieh, we came up with our Values as a group. Back then, there were about 40 of us. We broke up into groups of five to seven people and we played a couple of Innovation Games, starting with *Trim the Product Tree*.[80] As its name implies, this tool is meant to create a list of important product features, but it worked quite well for our purpose of coming up with a list of what was important to us as a group.

Our understanding back then is that these (uppercase) *Values* applied to the whole company, in any situation, at any time. These days, I believe that (lowercase) *values* are more relevant when associated with a process that makes them alive and relevant. Be careful to stay away from vague, feel-good words. For example, in the case of recruiting at Nearsoft we grade the candidate on each value on a one-to-four scale to discover each interviewer's perception of the candidate and have pointed conversations about big gaps, if any.

Process and values are the yin and yang of effective execution. If you can't identify what makes a process valuable, then you are probably following a bureaucratic procedure.

Nearsoft Values ended up describing the qualities we wanted future Nearsoftians to have.[81] As luck would have it, *Teamwork, Leadership, Commitment, Smart and gets things done,* and *Long-term relationships* are as appealing and meaningful to our clients as they are to us because they describe the qualities we both look for in people.

Over time, other things come up regularly during the recruiting process,[82] like curiosity and resourcefulness. A comment like, "… I didn't learn about it because I didn't need it for my job," usually is a red flag. Another characteristic that comes up often is whether or not the candidate is a self-learner, an autodidact. Did she talk about things that she had learned on her own or by reaching out to more experienced people? Or were all her answers some version of, "they didn't send me to that course?" By now, "curiosity" and "autodidact" have become part of our de facto values of the hiring process.

We use our values-as-checklist at the end of the interview process, during what we call our Thumbs meeting. At this meeting, all the people who talked to the candidate get together and each interviewer grades the candidate on a 1-4 scale along two axes: skills and cultural alignment.

Most of the time, all the interviewers line up, but every so often, we have trouble coming to an agreement. And that's where having these Values is precious. Are we talking about leadership or commitment issues? Was it apparent that she didn't care about long-term relationships? Every so often, somebody says, "but, she doesn't have a degree!" even though it's not in our list of Values. But that is easily dealt with, the same way I was disabused of that "requirement" a while back. Did she know her tech stuff? Did she come up short against any of our values? Didn't she demonstrate curiosity? Doesn't the fact that she learned a bunch of skills pretty much by herself show that she is smart and resourceful? Then, what's with "a degree?"

There may be a very short list of core values that apply to the whole company, but I am not so sure anymore; in fact, I doubt it. On the other hand, I am very sure that each key process needs a checklist associated with it that defines what makes it meaningful and why we are doing this, it defines what makes it valuable. The process of coming up with these values, itself, provides clarity and creates a common commitment to the goals of a given process, and will help to prevent them from becoming a bureaucratic checklist.

In our new RADICAL company it would make sense to experiment to find values for key processes.

9
RADICAL
DISTRIBUTION

FOR AT LEAST 100 years, many have been aware of the problems with our model of private, oligarchic ownership. As we've mentioned, the followers of Marx tried one way of solving it, but that didn't work. Others, like Olivetti in Italy and others in Europe, tried the paternalistic approach, but that didn't last. Still others have championed the cooperative model of equal ownership, but that has not taken the world like fire, either.

On the other side of the coin, the joint-stock business, a capitalist invention, has been very, very financially successful. That's the system where businesses sell shares of themselves to investors. The financial markets are all about this and so is Venture Capital. Having individuals pool their money to fund big projects is one of the foundations of capitalism.

For example, a baker wants to make a giant cake (the joint-stock company). Myself and others (investors) buy the ingredients in exchange for a share of the cake's sale price. "I bought him sugar for $1 and I got $1.50 in return when the cake was sold." Or maybe I can't wait until the cake is sold, so I sell my share of the cake to you, another investor, for $1.25; later, you get $1.50 when the cake is sold. It's a sweet deal all around, and you don't have to be very particularly wealthy to be part of this, but you have to have money that you don't mind losing if the cake doesn't sell or is sold for less than expected.

But what about the baker's helpers? They don't have any money to spare and they get their wages, but none of the extra wealth that they helped create. If he is feeling generous, maybe the baker can give them some of his shares. Or the investors are willing to chip in to buy shares that would go to the helpers. Or maybe the government can dictate that a percentage of the sale is divided equally among the workers. Note that in all these cases,

- Some people, one or a few, decide for others. They choose what and how much to give (*i.e.*, the government counts as one person).
- The worth of each share is static, fixed at the beginning of this process and way before the cake is baked.
- The number of shares the workers get, if they get any, is arbitrary.
- The government mandate may be egalitarian but not likely equitable.

The option of letting the workers decide is anathema to the FIAT mindset. It is simply unthinkable and too scary to be considered for more than a fleeting moment. "It would be too chaotic and paralyzing." But labor is as important as capital in making new things happen.

The Distribution mechanism we describe below makes ownership decentralized and dynamic. It supports egalitarian and equitable wealth sharing based on contribution. And it is scalable.

Rosedale Distribution

Rosedale Distribution is our name for a practice that I first heard from entrepreneur Philip Rosedale, [83] founder of Linden Labs, High Fidelity, and several other companies in between. He came up with this scheme in 2005 when Linden had about 50 employees. It goes like this,

- As the company grows, a small amount of cash and shares are put out for distribution every month.
- Every member gets, say, $1,000, an equal portion of the wealth the company generated.
- People don't get to keep these goodies for themselves: they get to distribute them to other members.
- They give it to anybody they feel has contributed the most during the month. Each person knows best who has contributed.
- Each person decides how much to give to whom based on whatever criteria "feels right" at that time.
- Each member gets to have a direct impact on company ownership.

A company in Argentina, Manas, does something very similar. [84]They knew nothing of Rosedale's system and independently came up with a similar system. This goes to show that many of us are moving in the same direction, albeit haphazardly.

RADICAL Distribution

The RADICAL Distribution is based on the Rosedale Distribution. In both cases, everyone has a direct hand in doing something that is usually reserved for owners—wealth and ownership distribution—and they get in the habit of doing so. And like the Rosedale Distribution, the process is scalable. Ten thousand people can distribute wealth and ownership the same way that a handful of people can.

Instead of cash or stocks, RADICAL Distribution uses a dimensionless unit we call a RAD. Whereas money and stock shares has a *fixed* value, RADs *factor* value through them. Whereas stocks represent a fixed percentage of the company *forever*, RADs represent a dynamic *percentage* of ownership at each cycle. And they represent any kind of contribution, not just financial. In fact, as an accounting tool, RADs account for the uncountable.

Like the Rosedale Distribution, RADICAL Distribution has an "egalitarian" component and an "equitable" component. The egalitarian piece is that everyone gets an equal number of RADs which represent an equal portion of what they have created together. Co-owners then get to distribute these RADs according to their individual judgement. Each decides what is an equitable number of RADs to give to other co-owners as recognition for their contributions. The value of the whole emerges from the judgement of the many.

A few important observations,

- RADs are not a currency.
- RADs are issued before there is revenue because contributions happen regardless of revenue.
- The giving criteria is completely up to each person, although we can agree to some explicit guiding criteria to start with. In any case, at Distribution Retrospectives

new criteria are fleshed out and harvested as an optional guideline.

- RADs represent *dynamic* ownership. One month you may give me all your RADs, but the next month you may not give me any.

- The absolute number of RADs allocated to me either stays the same or goes up at every distribution. If I had 100 RADs last cycle and I get 50 this cycle, my total number of RADs goes to 150. If I don't get any this cycle, my total number of RADs stays at 100.

- On the other hand, my percentage of the total could go up, stay the same, or go down at every Distribution. If my 100 RADs represented 10% of the total last cycle and I get 150 RADs this cycle, then my percent ownership went up to 12.5%; if I get 100 new RADs, my percentage stays at 10%; if don't get any new RADs, my percentage goes down to 5%.

- To calculate your percentage ownership, divide the number of RADs you have been allocated by the total number of allocated RADs.

- When money, or time, or whatever else is disbursed later, it is done as a function of the number of RADs each person owns. If you have accumulated 200 RADs and I have 100, then you'll get twice as much as me of whatever is being factored through the RADs.

There probably are many ways of doing this,

- Every cycle each member gets to distribute a number of RADs as they see fit. For example, if you get 100 RADs this month, you may give fifty to Adrian, 30 to Jose, and 20 to me.

- Alternatively, co-owners might get one RAD per day. They could then allocate fractions of this one RAD. One tenth to Adrian, 0.01 to Jose, and 0.001 to me.

- We may have Distribution events once a month, where everybody participates. Alternatively, you may do your allocations daily and I may do them once a month. Or maybe you start daily and then skip a few days before you allocate again.
- Your unallocated RADs may disappear every day or they may accumulate for a month or a year.

As always, you'll have to experiment to see what works for you.[85]

We hope it's enough to get started.

Scalability

Because Distributions are decentralized, scalability is not an issue. Everybody has a very detailed and nuanced perspective on the contribution of a subset of people. And, yes, this view is biased, but, as Phil Rosedale points out, "… if you let everybody in the company impose their own bias on the situation but you give them all an equal amount of money, all the biases cancel each other out and the only coherent signal that remains is: I want the company to be around"[86]

People are the best judges of *who* should be recognized and *what* should be recognized as a contribution,

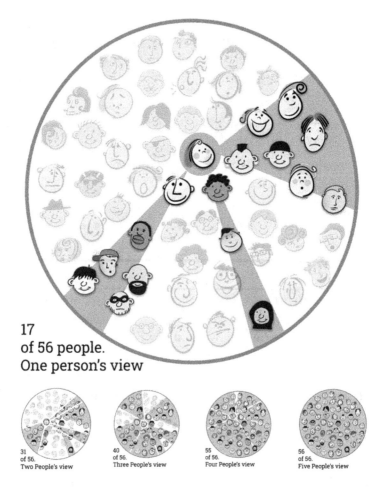

17
of 56 people.
One person's view

31
of 56.
Two People's view

40
of 56.
Three People's view

55
of 56.
Four People's view

56
of 56.
Five People's view

As people share and grant each other RADs, they learn the value of what they've built together at a visceral level. People will be encouraged to learn to communicate better ("It ain't bragging if you've done it"[87]). They will learn from their peers to value their accomplishments. They will learn to talk about their failures, what they've learned from them, and how it can be valuable to others. Phil Rosedale, again, puts his finger on the key point, "If you know your peers are going to judge you each quarter freely and give money to you, you'll probably work at being more transparent."[88]

Equality vs Equity

After we had written about RADICAL Distributions, we ran into a study by DeVoe and Iyengar where they conclude that, "people view it as less fair to distribute resources equally when the allocated resource invokes the market by being a medium of exchange than when the allocated resource is a good that holds value in use."[89] In other words, giving everybody $12 regardless of contribution is more likely to be seen as unfair than giving everybody a dozen carrots. The dozen carrots can only be eaten, whereas the $12 can be saved, used to pay credit card debt, or used to buy something online. As a fact, at Nearsoft the way of distributing Earned Dividends (*i.e.*, money) is no longer in equal portions because of a general sense that it was "unfair" to do it that way; it may change again in the future.

RADICAL Distributions let each co-owner allocate RADs as they see fit. Equalify is not the goal, equity is. e resulting allocations will most likely not be equal, but they'll be equitable according to 1) what each co-owner recognizes as a contribution and 2) how valuable that contribution is. Every co-owner has a different view of what equitable is and will be able to express it in tangible ways through RAD allocations.

New Features

In the Rosedale Distribution, 1) the criteria for "what's equitable" remains inside people's heads, and 2) it's all about individuals, not teams. To address these issues, we added two new features to RADICAL Distributions,

- *Retrospectives.* To make the Distribution criteria available to others RADICAL Distributions include a Retrospective step.

- Feedback. Anybody who wants to can call for a feedback session after a Distribution. It can help resolve latent tensions, correct wrong impressions, and get better results in the future.

- *Banners.* To give everybody an opportunity to recognize teams, we came up with Banners. These can also be used to represent special accomplishments, projects, investments, causes, communities, etc.

Retrospectives

To address the lack of transparency around criteria, RADICAL Distribution adds a retrospective step. At a RADICAL Retrospective, members discuss the criteria they used to allocate RADs. Participation in these Retrospectives is voluntary and members can share as much as they'd like of their criteria.

This may range from "I gave mine to people who worked with me on…" to "I was feeling depressed and the person I gave most of my RADs to was there for me." These criteria are documented and published for others to learn from and consider them at future distributions, if they wish. Over time, this serves as a training mechanism for members, particularly the new ones who are not yet used to doing "owner things." It does not prevent people from making their own decisions, but it serves as a guide.

Another approach is to define a starting criteria. An example of this is what social entrepreneur and consultant Dr Christine McDugall calls a Synergistic Audit. This audit consists of six dimensions, including matter, currency, tools & artifacts, know-how, warm data,[90] and well-being. The value of following a framework like this is to bring out what's important to each member and make sure it doesn't go unnoticed.

Feedback Sessions

There has been a lot of research on the dynamics of power and status in relationships.

Power is the ability to realize one's interest. Status is behavior that enhances another person's stature. Power exacts compliance and status invites cooperation. Both are "equally stable and predictable" social structures, according to social psychologist Michael R A Chance.[91]

RADICAL Distributions work because people like to give (power) and receive (status). In as much as the giving and receiving of RADs is a form of recognition, Distributions "will reflect on one's own power and status... and on the power and status of the other."[92]

By giving, my own power goes up (*i.e.*, without diminishing anybody else's power). Everybody in the company gets to experience the joy of giving and the jolt of power that goes with it. In the status dimension, it is a bit more complicated. If you get more than you expected, everything's peachy and you're overjoyed, "There appears to be nothing like the joy of unexpected rewards."[93] But if you get less than expected, "anger and depression can both result from an episode of status loss."[94] Instead we can turn these situations into learning opportunities.

One way to do this is to have anybody who wants to call for a feedback session after a Distribution. In particular, people who didn't get anything or significantly less than they expected would want to do this. It might be difficult to hear the feedback, but it's the way to grow. It can help resolve latent tensions, correct wrong impressions, and get better results in the future.

Banners

At Nearsoft, anybody can make up whatever title they want for themselves. However, that's not the same as being recognized by others. I confused the two for a long time.

Recognition is really important to both the giver and the receiver. Whether as individuals or as a team, having our accomplishments recognized by others is very important and precious to people.

Distribution Banners can stand for teams, special accomplishments, communities, new products, etc.

Teams	Teams can be represented by a Banner. "re: Recognize our IT support team for how they handled the storm."
Special Accomplishment	"Margot deserves to be recognized for stewarding the creation of our training platform."
Community	For example, a "No Noise" banner could fund a sound barrier around a noisy factory. A "River Walk" banner could fund a clean up and beautification of a stream that runs nearby. One could even fund a local vet hospital to help it recover from a fire.

Experimental Projects	At one point Google got a lot of coverage for their policy of allowing everybody to use 20% of their time to work on side projects and things like Google News came out of it. That was a generous policy given by the FIAT owners, but the same owners later took it away.

For a RADICAL company the equivalent thing would be to put up a "20%" Banner and co-owners could allocate RADs to it as they see fit. Or more specifically, a "Google News" Banner could fund that specific project. |
| Investments | In FIAT businesses the owners can decide whether or not to, say, purchase a new office building. Maybe it is done as a wise investment, or maybe it has more to do with ego, like a pharaoh's pyramid.

In a RADICAL company, anybody can put up a "New building" Banner and allow co-owners to contribute to the funding of it or not. |

See Earned Dividends, an Example for more details.

Distribution Transparency

"Will everybody know who I gave RADs to and how many?"
"Will they know how many I got and from whom?"

The fear behind these questions is not irrational: disclosing your salary can get you in big trouble at a FIAT business. It's a taboo subject and you may have even convinced yourself that the secrecy is for your own good. No wonder some people are fearful about it.

These kinds of questions are very similar to the ones that sometimes come up when we tell people that at Nearsoft our salaries are open. As of this writing, there are over 450 Nearsoftians and I can count on one hand the number of people who have voiced concerns over this. Long story short, at Nearsoft we've never had to hide anybody's salary.

We don't think that RADICAL Distributions will work without complete transparency. In theory, the allocator and recipient could block their identity or the number of RADs allocated, but that is fear speaking, limiting our options. We don't think that anything less than full disclosure will work.

Of course, you'll have to figure out what works for you, but hiding any of this information is likely to turn out to be a failure.

Accounting for the Unaccountable

RADs represent many things other than simple financial value. They are not beans, but they can be counted.

The RADs you have represent how other people feel about you and how they value your contributions. If you are making us miserable, you'll probably get fewer RADs from us; if you are helping us thrive, you'll likely get more. If you do something that goes against our Impact, "but, hey, it makes money," you'll get less RADs; if instead you introduce a way to make money *and* strengthen our alignment, you'll get more RADs.

Maybe I gave you RADs because you noticed that I was down and you talked to me and helped me get over a personal crisis. Or noticed that you always make yourself available to help others in the team. Or it may indicate that you are a very effective coach, gentle and inspirational at the same time.

In short, RADs account for the uncountable, they measure the immeasurable.

10
CO-OWNERSHIP &
CO-MANAGEMENT

A FIAT HIERARCHY makes it impossible to co-manage or co-own a business. With a FIAT hierarchy in place, co-management is at best temporary, at worst all but lip service. If you have a boss who can fire you, or demote, or otherwise punish you, you will hold back on what you say. Your ability to make decisions and take action will be very, very restricted. A FIAT boss can cancel any decision that a subordinate makes. So what if you and your peers spent hours interviewing a candidate and after a five minute conversation with the candidate he says, "I don't think he's a good fit." The boss made a decision and that's all you need to know.

The current state of Agile is the canonical example of this. The original idea was to have software developed by a complete, self-managed team. But even with the best intentions, it is impossible to sustain a self-managed team within a FIAT hierarchy. The daily standup meeting has turned into a reporting meeting not because the boss is a bad person but because *his job is to report up* the hierarchy, to *his* boss. It doesn't matter that the Agile team discovered a major obstacle, you can take it out of scope because sales promised that feature already, and... who's going to tell the CEO? Delivering "value to our customer" plays second fiddle to face saving up and down the chain of command. There are a few pockets of co-managed Agile teams here and there, but they're very fragile. Mostly they revolve around an enlightened boss who is clever enough to hide it and protect it. Once the enlightened boss is out of the picture, that's the end of the experiment, regardless of results. That's because the FIAT hierarchy values the perception of control above all else.

Co-ownership, too, is blocked by the FIAT hierarchy. Cooperatives are a good example of that. For example, Mondragon, the biggest co-op on the planet, is run by a traditional FIAT hierarchy. Even though workers are the "owners," they have little participation in strategic decisions. At Mondragon and other cooperatives, the workers are well taken care of, but they are not owners. This type of "ownership" is what Dr Rosen calls *symbolic ownership*, enjoying financial benefits but nothing else. Co-ownership requires participation in strategic and structural decisions that affect the overall company. It's not only about knowing how to "read the books," but getting involved in decisions that have an impact on said books.

To work, ownership must be decentralized and broadly distributed to everybody who contributes to the company.

Co-Ownership

In a conversation with author and self-management coach Chuck Blakeman, I once bemoaned the fact that co-management by itself was way too dependent on "enlightened monarchs," owners who are seriously committed to co-management. But co-management ends when the benign boss walks off the stage.

Chuck certainly is one of the enlightened ones. He has led co-management "in twelve businesses, in eight industries, on four continents."[95] These days, among other things, he trains and coaches people on their co-management journey.

Back when we had that conversation I couldn't think of any way of doing co-management without a benevolent boss. Without co-ownership, co-management happens "at the pleasure of" the FIAT owner and a new, not-so-enlightened owner can easily revert to traditional FIAT management. No matter how you slice it, the owner is the boss,

Jack Riminton
@jackrim1

Replying to @3dfordesigners

To 'flat management' etc I always follow the money, who's got the biggest equity stake? There's your boss

2:20 PM · Feb 5, 2020 · Twitter for iPhone

96

Co-ownership removes co-management's dependence on an owner. It replaces FIAT ownership and decentralizes the kind of power and distributes its power. Everyone who contributes to the company is a co-owner of it and co-management happens at *their* pleasure. They are not symbolic owners and their voices actively count when it comes to reserved-for-owners decisions.

At home, people behave a certain way because it *is* their home and they *own it* beyond the legal sense. They belong there. They feel entitled to ask questions and know what's going on. They feel responsible for fixing things. Each member of the household is accountable to the others.

At work, FIAT owners behave similarly, with a sense of entitlement and responsibility. Everybody else is working for a wage. Full-time, part-time, or on-demand. Salaried, per hour, per widget, or on commission. Even well-paid superstars and big time execs. All of them work "at the pleasure of" the FIAT owner. FIAT ownership is the reason why our businesses are so inefficient and make us all miserable. Co-ownership aims to break this cycle by decentralizing ownership and making people co-owners of the companies they embody. It leverages ownership, a foundation of capitalism, and makes it more widely available. It makes people active participants in financial and strategic decision making, not just the recipients of financial benefits.

ESOPs and co-operatives are not co-ownership because they focus on the money end of things but say nothing about who runs things or how. "More money for us!" is not sufficient. Money may be what keeps me awake at night if I don't have enough of it, but it's not what makes me spring out of bed in the morning. And it's definitely not what fills me with pride and satisfaction at the end of the day.

Co-ownership is about having everybody in a company walk around with a sense of entitlement, responsibility, and accountability about their workplace. Because. They. Own. It.

What Does an Owner Own

These are some of the decisions that a FIAT owner may make (or has veto power over),

Fate of the company	Are we going to sell the business? Are we going to buy another business? Are we going to merge with another business?
Strategy	What business should we be in? Do we stay in that niche? Do we expand to an adjacent area? How do we position the business, our products?
Hiring and firing	Who gets hired? How much/little can I offer? Who gets fired? Do I pay any severance?
How to deal with bad times?	What to do during times of flat or negative growth? Do we borrow? How much? Do we take capital investments? How much and for what percentage of the company? Do we lay off people? How many? Who?

In addition, the owner also has the final word on these decisions,

Investments	Are we going to grow our current business? Are we going to invest in a new or adjacent business? Do we borrow money? How much and from whom? How much will we spend on training?

Capital Allocation	What do we do with this year's profit? Do I, as the owner, take it all or most of it? Do we grow our operations next year? Do we reserve some for Earned Dividends? Do we fund a new office? What about shares for merit?
Share distribution	Do I give/sell shares of the business to anybody? How many? For how much? Who? When? What's the criteria?
Wealth Extraction	How much is reserved for the owners? Should we implement Profit Sharing? How do we handle salaries, raises? Do we pay for parties, offsites?

We have been conditioned to believe that "regular" people can't deal with these issues, only the gifted amongst us can and these gifted people deserve the rewards of their special talent. So it must have taken me a long time to become gifted because it took me six businesses before the seventh was financially successful. Or maybe I was gifted all along, but it took me a while to "embrace my gift," so to speak. Or maybe it had to do with some unresolved sexual fantasy (remember Freud?). But, "talent is overrated. Skill is acquirable." [97]

The reality is that I *learned* about these things. There was no "gift" involved, that is, other than my partner, Roberto, from whom I still learn a lot. I've been very lucky and privileged, but I am not *that* special. And I am not saying that out of false modesty. I am full of myself and I think the world of me, but I still learn new lessons every day from those around me. And it wasn't my magic that made Nearsoft successful, it took a lot of work from a lot of people.

So maybe the people whose labor makes a company grow and thrive, maybe they could learn what they need to learn about ownership to have a voice in it and make even more significant contributions. And maybe the whole thing about the "gift" is a convenient mythology that's been around for a long time and we accept as fact, even when it isn't.

Co-ownership gives every member the chance to learn to become an owner in every sense of the word. Not everybody will start at the same level, not everybody will be equally interested, and not everybody will learn at the same rate. But co-ownership provides the training ground for members to develop as owners.

Transparency and Decentralization

Jack Stack, an enthusiastic champion of Open-Book Management, makes the point that he had to learn these things on his own because the company he worked for didn't think he was trustworthy enough, even though he was a boss. "You begin to realize that this is not rocket science, that I could understand these metrics... I'd get angry at the company I worked for because in the 14 years I worked there, the company didn't think I could understand those metrics..."[98]

By whatever name it goes, need-to-know, confidentiality, etc., lack of transparency is the enclosure of information, knowledge, and know-how. As Stack discovered, transparency is required in order to make decisions. "To build a company that is really productive... by teaching people the metrics of a great company."[99]

Earlier, in the late 1970s, Ricardo Semler had a similar realization at SEMCO: regular people, with a basic education could learn to understand the company's finances. "All financial information at Semco is openly discussed... workers have unlimited access to our books... with the labor unions that represent our workers, we developed a course to teach everyone, even messengers and cleaning people, to read balance sheets and cash flow statements."[100]

Other things, like hiring and firing, can be handled by regular people on their own, without a boss-as-babysitter. But bosses have to impose themselves on the process even when it adds friction to it and makes it less efficient. After all, that's their job.

The Case for Co-ownership

From the onset, Nearsoft has been a grand experiment where we've tried out lots of ways to co-managed as peers. We also took a couple of steps into what I recognize now as co-ownership (*e.g.*, changing the distribution method of Earned Dividends). However, co-ownership had no name and no recognizable shape then and we didn't get far enough on that path.

Ownership is something that most of us never learn about. Particularly, ownership of a productive asset, like a business. Homeownership is not the same as being the owner of an asset that actively generates wealth.

Without co-ownership, co-management is tenuous and always "at the pleasure of" the FIAT owners. No matter how well-intended these folks are, it all comes to an end when they are no longer the owners. Co-ownership is the way out of that trap. It does not depend on taxes or new laws or other government actions. It is not a call for the end of Capitalism. What's radical about co-ownership is that it does require a serious reshaping of ownership, one of the foundations of Capitalism. The other foundation is the market.

The Not-So-Hidden Hand

As Adam Smith laid out in *The Wealth of Nations*, the market is a decentralized pricing apparatus. That may be so in theory, but in practice it is not. Capital tends to concentrate into fewer and fewer hands and financial markets are not the level-playing field we believe they are.[101] "Even if the outcome of every transaction is chosen by a fair coin flip, many such sales and purchases will inevitably result in all the wealth falling into the hands of a single person—leading to a situation of extreme inequality."[102]

Bernard Lietaer, an economist, author, and professor, studied monetary systems. With co-author Jacqui Dunne he makes a convincing case that this imbalance has a lot to do with interest bearing currency. This transfer of wealth occurred independently of the cleverness or industriousness of the participants, attributes often assumed to account for differences in income,

> "Because of the upward concentration of wealth caused by interest, there was a transfer of wealth from the bottom 80 percent of the population to the top 20 percent, especially the top 10 percent, due exclusively to the interest feature of the monetary system used.

> "This transfer of wealth occurred independently of the cleverness or industriousness of the participants, attributes often assumed to account for differences in income. This, in turn, makes a mockery of the very concept of free markets, as no one is really free in such a system."[103]

You don't have to go far for the evidence: the richest 62 people own half of the world's wealth.[104] Decisions are made for the sake of more "possessions or riches" and little else. We can try and change the monetary system or we can decentralize our ownership model. We think that the latter option is the most practical and the most effective. As company ownership spreads and the decision-making authority and habits that comes with it broadens, we all will be better for it.

Full Ownership

As we've said, being an owner is far more than just being a financial beneficiary. True owners take an active part in running the company, including financial and strategy decisions.

There have been attempts to broaden ownership, but they all end up not going far enough. Here is our analysis of the better known ones,

ESOPs	An ESOP provides the legal basis for approximating universal equity ownership. But the ESOP must be set to really operate with the full participation of the co-owners and that is almost never the case. New Belgium Brewery came closest and then it got acquired by Kirin.
Open Book Management	Open Book Management provides financial transparency and so it seems to fit the co-ownership model. It illustrates that transparency is not just making the numbers available and posting them on the walls. People need to know how to read these numbers and how to figure out what it means to them as well as to the company.
	But it doesn't require equity ownership or any other real ownership. People learn to read the books, but they don't get to participate in the decisions that shape them.

| Co-operatives (or LCAs) | Every member owns an equal piece of the co-op, but they don't necessarily participate in strategic decisions. One member, one vote is irrelevant without co-management. What matters is that members get to participate in shaping the questions, not just voting for A or B.

In the RADICAL co-ownership model not all co-owners own the same percentage; their fellow co-owners decide the value of their contributions. |

For a more extended analysis, see *Not Quite Co-ownership*.

The Tragedy of Symbolic Ownership

In 2014, Fagor,[105] the business that launched what's today known as Mondragon,[106] was on a financial losing streak. Its market was changing dramatically and other appliance manufacturers had closed down or were about to. Management felt that by injecting more capital they could outlast what they perceived as a temporary crisis.

In order to save the business, they proposed to use their internal capital to subsidize their operation. They put it to a vote, and it was approved by their worker-owners. What these nominal owners didn't seem to understand is that this "internal capital" included their social funds for retirement, savings, education, etc. Or maybe they did, but if management wanted to do it, then it must be OK.

Two years later, in 2016, Fagor threw in the towel and was shut down.

Most everybody got jobs with other Mondragon coops, but their Fagor social funds were wiped out. The worker-owners took to the streets to demonstrate against a decision that they themselves had voted for.

(Getty image)   IN DEFENSE OF OUR JOBS

It seems that these *workers* didn't really feel like *owners*. They went along with their management on the belief that they would be "taken care of." When it became obvious that was not the case, they felt betrayed and took to the streets.

Financial participation is *symbolic* ownership, not co-ownership.

Then, What Is Co-Ownership?

Co-owners have equity in their company and participate in financial and strategy decisions. Anything short of this is not co-ownership.

Many of the existing approaches may be a step in the right direction. They may be generous and possibly better than the norm. But without equity ownership and full participation in decision making it is not co-ownership. These programs, by themselves, don't represent co-ownership, only frustrating pieces of it.

As a counter-example, for as long as it remained independent the New Belgium Brewery combined an ESOP and Openbook Management practices to attain an effective form of co-ownership.

As we write this book, we can only think of W L Gore as a co-owned and co-managed company. Namasté Solar may be as well. BuurtzorgT is well on its way.[107] Founded by Jos de Blok and Nico Moleman in 2013, BuurtzorgT[108] grew very quickly and they needed capital to sustain its growth. Instead of the usual suspects, they found an investor that was open to Steward Ownership, "a viable alternative to shareholder-primacy ownership"[109] championed by Armin Steuernagel[110]

People Centered as Financial Strategy

In money-first terms, co-ownership is a financial winner, "A 2000 Rutgers study found that ESOP companies grow 2.3% to 2.4% faster after setting up their ESOP than would have been expected without it."[111] And so is co-management, "… world-class freedom-centered cultures based on the principles of organizational democracy… deliver 7x revenue growth (on average) compared to S&P 500 companies."[112]

When combining co-management with co-ownership, a company's financial performance could be much higher. For example, the NCEO reports that even companies with a limited form of participation "grow 8% to 11% per year faster with their ownership plans than they would have without them."[113]

In other words, putting people at the center of it all happens to be the smarter financial strategy, too. Go figure.

Co-Management

Co-management means that you and your co-workers are responsible for creating a company that works for you. There is no "packaged" solution, only a lot of work and lots of experimentation to figure out what works for each unique group of people.

In a FIAT business, you just ask the boss. In a co-managed company, you don't have a boss and you and your co-workers have to come up with the answers. Be careful not to replace a FIAT hierarchy of individuals with a complex set of rules, agreements are not the same as a bureaucracy. There's no difference between "because I say so" and "because given the rules stated on page 32 of the 47 page document that you signed…" They are both FIAT, centralized mechanisms used to exert control.

There is no prescribed series of steps to get started. Find a community of people who have gone through it and learn from them. What's most important is that whatever you start with does not become dogma. You will make a pile of mistakes and that's the way it is. You will learn from each mistake more than from any instruction manual.

Ben *and* Jerry

Although we present co-ownership and co-management as two separate concepts, in reality they are inseparable, two sides of the same coin. Bonnie and Clyde. Sherlock Holmes and Dr Watson. Ben and Jerry. One without the other is not enough to impact the current narrative of our lives. One without the other does not have the sustained transformative effect we need in order to move forward.

In a FIAT company, co-management exists "at the pleasure of" the company's benevolent owner. Any form of financial benefit in a FIAT managed company is tenuous at best and, again, "at the pleasure of" the boss.

In the past, there have been a number of European companies that modeled and promoted wealth sharing (e.g., Olivetti in Italy, John Lewis and Scott Barder in the UK). They embraced a form of symbolic ownership but maintained a FIAT hierarchy firmly in charge.

The John Lewis Partnership in England is one of the best known examples of this. John Spedan Lewis, the son of the store's founder, turned all his shares of the company to a Trust owned by the company's employees, which he called partners. That made them the "owners" of the company and were entitled to receive the dividends that would have gone to Lewis and his family. However, he left the hierarchy of bosses intact. Lewis created a "highly elaborate governance structure comprising a series of forums, councils and internal publications"[114] as a check on management. Even then, over time the bosses have been in control of the company.

Earnest Bader, founder of Scott Bader, sold all his and his family's shares to a company Trust and ceded all would-be dividends to the employees. But like John Lewis, he left a FIAT hierarchy in place. Here, too, the bosses have warped the company in their favor.

Less known is that Olivetti, the Italian typewriter company, "was once a model for workers' rights."[115] The system Adrianno Olivetti put in place survived him for 28 years but in the end it failed because it lacked co-ownership. Had that been in place, it might have prevented what eventually happened: a downstream CEO dismantled what Adriano called the co-determination system.

Gerard Endenburg, founder of Endenburg Electric, became the poster child of Sociocray and has been its most active promoter. He was inspired by the work of Kees Boeke and Beatrice Cadbury Boeke to put "Sociocratic Democracy"[116] to work at Endenburg Electric. Enderburg put his shares in a foundation for the benefit of employees. However, he also left in place a hierarchy. He hoped that "… the interlocking circles provide a check against its excesses."[117] Long story short, it didn't.

Further back, Wm. Filene Son's Co, a US retail empire, created the Filene Cooperative Association (FCA) in 1891,

> "Open to all interested employees, the FCA was a tool with which employees could advocate for improved work conditions. The FCA elected an eighteen-member executive council, which could overturn any store policy through a two-thirds vote. If management vetoed the proposed rule change, a unanimous vote of the FCA membership could overturn the veto….
>
> "Functioning independently of the store management, the body had the power to challenge and reverse the decisions of store supervisors. Further, the Filene brothers assured the FCA that employees could vote in any manner without fear of management reprisal."[118]

In 1901 the Filene Cooperative Association included an arbitration committee which adjudicated all dismissal cases and disciplinary actions. In 1902 the owners allocated shares to the Filene Cooperative Association. For its time, these actions were extremely progressive. Nevertheless they left a FIAT hierarchy in charge and Wm. Filene Son's Co was split apart, traded, and eventually made to disappear.

As Jack Quarter writes in *Beyond the Bottom Line*, as long as there is a boss around, he is "resistive, and often desires to hold onto its authority. At the same time employees, conditioned to a powerless role in decision making, have difficulty expressing themselves, even when given the opportunity to do so."[119]

Co-ownership *and* co-management need each other to last.

Braided Voices

The combination of co-ownership and co-management support each co-owner's own voice. Every co-owner has the same "right" to speak up on a subject, any subject. But not a herd of grunts but as an aligned team of people. Having listened to those who speak, the group will have a chane to align with the voice that represents "the highest level of consciousness," to use Laloux' terminology or the highest "psychic force" as Mary Parker Follet put it 100 years earlier.[120] This is not a single voice, but the integration of all contributions made. One says, another adds, the other riffs on the combination. Their voices braid, it resonates, and the group moves. The rhythm of the human voice, the melody of conversation, the lyrics that come forth: that's the group dance and that is what meaning and belonging are all about.

For one, this opens the door to real novel innovation to come from anybody, not just a select few. If you start to implement it and it becomes obvious that it is not going to work, the co-owners working on it will know and pull the red flag. If it looks like it's going to work, the co-owners will probably make it better and get out the door sooner.

The boss limits the level of consciousness that a group can attain because his voice is the only one that is heard. It is the only one that counts because no matter what, employees must follow the boss' directions. We need a system that unblocks the group's "capacity for independent action," a system that doesn't depend on an extraordinary boss. We need a system where everyone is a co-owner and there's no set limit to where the group can reach working together.

11
TWENTY-FIRST CENTURY COMMONS

RADICAL Framework

IT WOULD BE great if we had a framework for building a RADICAL company. It would guide us as individuals, as teams, and as an organization. It would allow us to figure out if we are making progress or not. Well, the framework we describe below comes as close as we can hope.

For the RADICAL Framework, we started from the work of political economist Elinor Ostrom, the first woman to win the Nobel Prize in Economics. Ostrom's award was based on her work with Commons, or as she called them Common Pool Resources. She framed her findings as eight Core Design Principles,

1. Boundaries of users and resource are clear

2. Congruence between benefits and costs
3. Users had procedures for making own rules
4. Regular monitoring of users and resource condition
5. Graduated sanctions
6. Conflict resolution mechanism
7. Minimal recognition of rights by government
8. Nested enterprises

Ostrom's work showed that "people in small, local communities managed shared natural resources, such as pastures, fishing waters, and forests" and the successful ones agreed on rules "for how these are to be cared for and used in a way that is both economically and ecologically sustainable."[121]

As we see it, RADICAL companies are the Commons of the twenty-first century. Both Commons and RADICAL companies are managed by the people who embody them (co-management) and in both cases they dynamically share the benefit of their bounties (co-ownership).

For RADICAL companies, we've recast her Core Design Principles as,

1. Clearly defined boundaries
2. Balanced contributions and benefits
3. Inclusive Decision Making
4. Monitoring
5. Graduated sanctions
6. Conflict management
7. Right to co-manage
8. Polycentric governance

Core Design Principles

Here's our take on Ostrom's Core Design Principles and how they apply to RADICAL companies,

#1. Clearly defined boundaries

Clear, explicit definition of 1) what determines who can be a member of a team or a company, 2) who has rights to extract wealth from the company, and 3) the company's constitutional framework that specifies what it is about.

This Core Design Principles applies both to the company as a whole and to each team. Who is and is not a member is probably the most important criterion that needs to be made explicit.

At a company level, a member is anybody who contributes to its Impact, Purpose, and Mission. Whether that's their "day job" or something somebody does once, if they end up contributing to the company, then they are members. Their level of contribution is determined by other members at every Ownership Distribution event.

For example, a capital investor can be a member this way if the investor helps bring in new customers. Said investor can also be a member if she offers valuable advice given on her experience and skills. Her investment will get paid back handsomely, but it's her contributions that make her a member and others' recognition of these contributions (via RAD allocations) make her a co-owner.

Each team is responsible for accepting, and rejecting, individual members. Again, these could be full time members of the team or more casual contributors. It's a good practice, and a lot healthier, to make that criterion explicit and not have it drift from one day to the next. It can expand or change as need be, but having it be explicit is very important.

For example, at Nearsoft the issue of self-learning comes up often at some point in the interview process. People feel strongly about wanting to team up with others who are curious and pick up new stuff on their own or with the help of more knowledgeable people. They definitely cringe away from folks who simply complain that, "they didn't train me on that." Being an autodidact is definitely valuable to Nearsoftians and shapes the boundary of who they want to team up with.

#2. Balanced contributions and benefits

The balance of contributions, recognition, and other rewards must be trusted as fair and equitable.

As Dr Paul Atkins of PROSOCIAL points out, "Most people have a strong sense of equity that is violated when someone receives benefits disproportionate to their contributions. Perceived fairness is essential for high group performance."[122]

And not just people. The video below shows the capuchin monkey on the left vigorously objecting to his getting a (low value) cucumber while his neighbor on the right gets a (high value) grape *for doing the same task.*

123

They've run this experiment with dogs, birds, and chimpanzees with the same results.

For RADICAL companies, the insistence on transparency makes it possible to fully support this Core Design Principle. Any co-owner can figure if contributions and benefits are, to them, fairly balanced or not.

Contributions are relative to the group's alignment (*e.g.*, Mission, Purpose, and Impact). It could be introducing a new practice, improving an existing one, or doing something, anything, with broad positive impact.

If you do something that moves our Purpose forward, you'd like to be recognized and rewarded for it, as would we. This may be an attaboy from a colleague, public fireworks, or more tangibly, a RAD allocation. The important thing is that the act and the reward be transparent and balanced. Capricious and arbitrary rewards is the kind of thing that happens more often than not in FIAT managed companies. The boss' favorite always gets applauded for even the simplest things, while the amazing deeds of others can easily be dissed because "the boss doesn't like you."

For example, take budget allocation. The process for defining and allocating budgets has to be transparent and equitable. In a FIAT managed business, the boss' pet project gets the big budget while everybody else fights for the crumbs. In a RADICAL company, the budgeting process is in members' hands and it is transparent.

#3. Inclusive Decision Making

Anybody affected by a decision must participate in the process of making that decision.

As we interpret this, this is one of the earliest practices that we made explicit at Nearsoft: anybody impacted by a decision must participate in that decision in some way, shape, or form. This has worked well for us.

It also implies that, for example, any group rules can be questioned at any time and possibly changed. Here again, the important thing is the discussion around the rule, its impact, and a resolution.

This includes getting ejected from a team. If you are thinking, "but… HR already does that," think again. In FIAT businesses, HR is responsible first and foremost for shielding the business and its top executives from lawsuits.[124] The HR Department is part of the bureaucratic control apparatus, "with its emphasis on methodical, rational-legal rules for direction, hierarchical monitoring, and rewards for compliance."[125]

So, when a boss wants to get rid of an employee, he dumps her on HR. Now that the decision has been made, HR's job is to dutifully inform said employee that she is going to be "put on a plan," a euphemism for, "you are going to get fired and we're going to do it all nice and legal so you can't sue us."

In a RADICAL company, before somebody is ejected from a team, she would have gotten plenty of feedback from her immediate team and others on what's not working. This doesn't happen consistently at Nearsoft, humans that we are, but when it does, the offending person listens to the feedback, applies as appropriate, or takes himself out of the team. In all Nearsoft's history, there have been only three cases when people had to be formally fired.

#4. Monitoring

People are responsible for and accountable to each other. Regular, formalized check-ins are essential to the health of a team. Reviews and feedback are valuable gifts.

In a RADICAL company, monitoring is pretty much shaped by what needs to be monitored. The dangers are, 1) not doing it or doing it surreptitiously, 2) doing it as a tool of control.

Like many people, I used to always interpret "monitoring" as a controlling act of supervision. Time clocks, hidden cameras, tracking technology. But monitoring doesn't have to be malicious or punitive.

Monitoring is key to coordination. Teams come together to work on shared tasks ("you hold it up while I nail it") and interdependent tasks ("let me know when you're finished nailing it, so I can paint it"). Something as simple as asking "Is this high enough?" is a form of monitoring, albeit an informal one.

Instead of leaving it to chance, monitoring needs to be made explicit. "We'll talk about all clients, including the ones we lost," rather than only talking about the successful ones. Fixing the time when we are going to do it is a good idea, too. "Every Monday at 10:30 AM Pacific." The specifics are not important and will be different for every team and whatever needs to be monitored. In fact, they will change as the team and circumstances change.

Trust has nothing to do with monitoring. In particular, having a monitoring process doesn't mean that we don't trust each other, and not having one does not mean that we trust each other unconditionally, either.

Monitoring is just another aspect of co-management.

My own tendency was to resist any form of monitoring, particularly with people I trust. "Let me know if anything comes up." But that doesn't work well enough. It puts too much of the onus on the individual to divine what, when, and how to report, or ask for a review, or solicit feedback. Monitoring is an "us" activity and one that we can't just dump on one of us.

Dr Paul Atkins, in PROSOCIAL, points out that to be successful, monitoring needs to be done consistently. Rich Barlett of Loomio, a "bossless organization," makes a similar observation about developing a regular rhythm.[126] In their view, the rhythm promotes accountability, focus, and agility.

#5. Graduated sanctions

Misconduct must be dealt with gradually, with sanctions that range from the gentle to the harsh. Just as important is to deal with sanctions in a transparent and balanced way and to do so decisively and quickly.

Ostrom observed that Commons worked better when sanctions went from gentle and good natured to unequivocal. This is no different for RADICAL companies. The same way that Core Design Principle #2 calls for a balance between contributions and benefits, this Core Design Principle calls for a balance between misconduct and sanctions.

You definitely must define a process for dealing with misdeeds. No good comes out of ignoring bad deeds. No matter how "little," the team must learn to point out any and all kinds of misconduct; people are usually pretty good at recognizing it, but voicing it is difficult, to put it mildly, because we often confuse feedback and criticism. Nevertheless, bringing them out and having a discussion about them is key. In fact, many times that's all it takes. This usually is enough of a "sanction" to correct the situation.

Whatever you do, moving quickly and decisively along that spectrum is very important. Letting the process stall is a slow and very painful death.

I've heard it said often enough that this is something that bosses do well and the rest of the people don't want to deal with it. Better for a boss to deal with the bad apple. From my own experience, bosses are generally worse at this than teams are. They ignore the misdeeds of their favorites, over-penalize the people they don't like, or they can't decide and leave the issues unresolved and festering. When they do act, it usually comes as a sudden rushing of the problem employee out the door. So, no, bosses are *not* especially good at this. Worst, how the bosses handle this is opaque to everybody else. People hear the nervous murmuring in the hallways, but they don't really know what or why really happened and are left to make up their own stories.

Having a system of graduated sanctions is very important, but, as Ostrom stated, just as important is to deal with sanctions in "a transparent and balanced way and to do so decisively and quickly."

#6. Conflict management

In order to resolve conflicts effectively and inexpensively (both emotionally and financially), recognizing and voicing conflicts is an essential skill.

Ostrom's original observation was about ways of dealing with conflict quickly and inexpensively, both financially and emotionally. Not jumping straight away to dragging neighbors through the legal system.[127]

However, for RADICAL companies, it is not just about resolving conflicts. Conflict has to be recognized and be brought out in the open before we can even talk about resolving it. Resolution is often not the hardest phase. More difficult than a resolution is training people to recognize conflict and getting people to point out the conflict and bring it out in the open.

From our first breath, we are taught to ignore conflict, walk away from it, go around it—we never learn to deal with it effectively. The usual pattern is to put up with it and put up with it until you can't take it anymore and then walk away or explode.

For RADICAL companies it is essential for people to learn to recognize conflict. What is this bringing up in me? Is it making me angry? scared? miserable?[128] It is even more important to learn to say it out loud without exploding, or walking away. Once the source of conflict is brought out to the open, its resolution becomes fairly self-evident.

For example, in the Nearsoft interview process, it sometimes happens that the candidate is clearly not aligned with our Values. When that happens we bring it out by plainly telling the candidate about our concerns. In my own experience doing interviews, I'll point out specific problems to the candidate and then we have a conversation that either resolves the issues on the spot, or we talk about specific areas to improve for next time (or we have her talk with another Nearsoftian).

Every conflict is a chance to learn about ourselves and about other members. Different people see the world differently, and resolving conflict is mostly a matter of aligning these differing views. There are people who are "a natural" at handling conflict well and with elegance. Most of us need training and practice. All of us can master it.

For RADICAL companies then, this Core Design Principle points out how important it is to learn to embrace conflict to make teams run well. The ability to recognize, voice, and resolve conflict is a must-have skill.

#7. Co-ownership as right to co-manage

Co-management is an integral part of RADICAL companies, not the special characteristic of isolated teams. Co-ownership is what gives a RADICAL company the right to co-manage.

For RADICAL companies, this is a given.

FIAT managed businesses can transform to co-management and gain the "right to co-manage," but it takes commitment and time. K2K Emocionando in Bilbao, Spain helps businesses go through that transformation and has done it successfully many, many times. They are proof that it is possible for FIAT businesses to metamorphosize into co-managed businesses, but it does take conviction and courage.

As we've pointed out, co-management is fragile and temporary if it depends on a benevolent owner. Co-ownership is what gives a RADICAL company the right to co-manage.

#8. Polycentric governance

RADICAL companies are decentralized and as such are governed policentrically. They also touch and are touched by many other adjunct communities including parent companies, subsidiaries, customers, candidates, industry peers, and the civil communities they are part of.

Ostrom observed that, "Appropriation, provision, monitoring, enforcement, conflict resolution, and governance activities are organized in multiple layers of nested enterprises." She was thinking of agencies that usually get involved with Common Pool Resources.

She originally called this principle *Nested Enterprises*. Later, Vincent Ostrom, her husband and an economist, suggested that this Core Design Principle be renamed Polycentric Governance, the shared governance of interdependent peer nodes. In fact, RADICAL companies themselves become polycentrically governed as they grow. They're decentralized organizations, with many decision making "centers" that come and go fluidly, as conditions require. What holds them together as "a company" is their alignment (*e.g.*, around Impact, Purpose, and Missions). In addition, RADICAL companies also interact with their customers, industry peers (*aka*, competitors), suppliers, candidates, and other communities they are part of.

Self-Assessment Tool

Based on the Ostrom Framework, we came up with this tool that a company can use to quickly assess itself against these design principles. This could be used to get a rough view of how well members feel their company is doing in each of these areas. The results give you a high level picture of their company's strengths and weaknesses. From there, you can figure out how to move the needle in one or more areas.

As a test, I did a quick, seat of the pants assessment of Nearsoft,

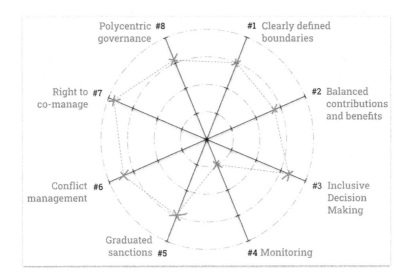

The results made it abundantly obvious that, in general, I felt that Nearsoft was weak when it came to Monitoring. I then spoke with a few Nearsoftians about it and they agreed that, in general, Monitoring was our weakest spot. I've always had a strong negative reaction to any "monitoring." As far as I was concerned, time clocks, hidden cameras, and any other tracking technologies were command-and-control tools. Bad stuff to stay away from.

Some of our early clients would ask us how we "tracked" people to make sure that they were "being productive." Around the time we started, there were body shops that were very proud of the fact that they took a snapshot of people's screens every few seconds as proof that their people were "working." As fads often go, prospects learned to ask us if we supported similar technology, but with a bit of prodding it was obvious that they also *knew* that this approach would be counterproductive. Eventually we learned to explain 1) that we didn't do that, 2) why we didn't do it, and 3) why they didn't want to work with businesses that relied on that type of sneaky behavior. That usually was enough to deal with the requisite question; and when it wasn't, it quickly made it clear that the prospect and us were not a good match.

In any case, that was monitoring to me: sneaky, intrusive, and punitive. Whenever the subject of monitoring came up I always had a million reasons why "we don't want to go there." It didn't occur to me then that monitoring is actually neutral. It doesn't have to be coercive and it doesn't have to lead to punishment. In fact, we "monitor" each other all the time, as when we "look out" for one another.

These days, we have a healthier view of monitoring at Nearsoft, but we have a lot of catch up to do.

12
CULTURAL
TRANSFORMATION

MOVING AWAY FROM a FIAT towards a RADICAL approach requires experimentation. Lots of it. As a matter of fact, the experimentation never ends. A culture emerges as people interact around those experiments. You can't transform a company's culture by lecturing, bringing outside experts, or turning to online courses. It is an honest-to-goodness paradigm shift and it is not easy to do.

The full transformation is two-fold: from FIAT ownership to co-ownership and from FIAT management to co-management. For a sustained transformation *you need both*.

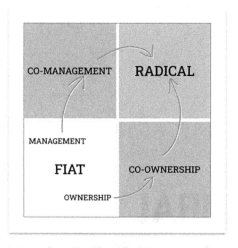

Co-management is enough to get people excited. For example, the various forms of Open Books Management have demonstrated that just knowing about the finances of a company is enough to get people engaged, at first. This is also why there's so much excitement about self-management today. What's missing, and it's absolutely required for the long term, is decentralized ownership.

Every company is different. There is no pre-packaged solution that will work for your company. And what works today won't necessarily work tomorrow. From my own experience, the way that Nearsoft operates today would have been overkill for the Nearsoft of 10 years ago and vice versa. In fact, every time we hire a new person, the company changes. You never know who is going to have a big impact, or when. I have been surprised by the impact some people have made, even some I originally thought were too "green" to make a difference.

We need to embrace experimentation and make learning a foundation of company culture. "Failure" is not failure unless you don't learn from it.

Zulema Salinas
@Zulema184

Replying to @Ridruejita

Todo cuenta al final. De lo malo se aprende y de lo bueno tomamos el aliento para seguir. Me siento afortunada. Un abrazo 🤗 🌹

Translate Tweet

4:02 AM · Aug 19, 2020 · Twitter Web App

129

Everything counts in the end. From failures we learn and from successes we take the encouragement to continue on. I feel lucky. Hugs.

Although it is not easy to do, in order to fully become an owner, you have to also become a fully functioning adult and grow out of your "good employee" (and "good boss") habits.

The Good Employee

"… even the knowledge and full conviction of a truth will not always immediately conquer inveterate habits and prejudices."

—*Viktor Frankl, Man's Search for Meaning*

The good employee appears docile. Does as she's told and never puts her boss in a bad light. Is OK when one of her bosses appropriates her ideas and presents them as his. Laughs at her bosses' jokes (because they are all funny). Always delivers on time or, if she can't, she is ready to explain why the delay is somebody else's fault.

An ambitious employee is very alert to any criticism and is quick to rebut it. Any comment short of positive is a criticism and may block her from moving up the ladder.

A hard working employee is always busy. Always supports her boss in emails and chat messages. Always writes down boss-friendly things (*i.e.*, because the boss will somehow find them and read them—after all, he's looking out for himself, too.)

A good boss is a good employee to her boss. And, of course, he expects his people to be good employees to him.

These are some of the habits and prejudices that we all pick up as we grow up in a FIAT world. Be obedient and don't make waves. At least, not so high that you'll be sent to the Principal's office.

We need to outgrow these habits as we transform into full adults. We know that this is possible with the minimum of support and encouragement, as I've seen at Nearsoft.

We Know Nothing

Before embarking on a cultural transformation, it'd be good to know what we really know, and we know little to nothing about alternatives to the FIAT world we live in. All we know today is the FIAT paradigm that has come together over a relatively long time and we really know nothing of what a different world would look and work like.

Social Science data can tell us *what is*, but not what it *could be*. There are a zillion studies about "the nature of people," but they really are about "the nature of people who were born and grew up in the FIAT system." We can't learn much about living on dry land by studying fish.

Take, for example, Robert Kegan's Socialized Mind.[130] According to Kegan, a psychologist, author, and consultant, the transformation from what he calls the Socialized Mind to the Self-Transforming Mind doesn't start until our 40s. But we suspect that it's a chicken-and-egg situation: it looks that way because that's what we are taught by word and by example throughout our lives. He's discovered a novel pattern in the data and that's great, but that data is about the FIAT system we live in, not about "the nature of" people. To this point, in the 1940s, "Education leaders presumed that 60% or more of all public school students lacked the *intellectual capability* for college work or even for skilled occupations."[131] They didn't make up the data, they reported on what they found back then. But what was true in the 1940s is laughable today.

The FIAT paradigm teaches us to remain dependent on the people "above" us, on those more powerful, and so Kegan's finding is not surprising. We suspect that as we get away from the FIAT paradigm, people will start to develop into self-transforming adults earlier and earlier. People in their 20s and 30s will shake their heads that we ever believed them incapable of developing as full adults before the age of 40.

More than likely, we will find that the socialized mind is always there and so is the self-transforming mind.[132]

When we started Nearsoft, we were told over and over that co-management would not work. "Where are you going to find enough people who can work without a manager? It's going to stunt your growth!" In the history of Nearsoft, from 2007 until the time of this writing, only three people have left the company because of "not enough structure." To date, over 450 Nearsoftians have done fine. It turns out that the people who take well to being treated as adults are neither special nor rare. Go figure.

What this tells us is that we know nothing about what the world will look like as we move away from the FIAT paradigm. Keep this in mind as you get well-intentioned advice from those "in the know."

Power Distance

In the early 1970s, Geert Hofstede came up with his Cultural Dimensions Theory based on his worldwide survey of IBM employees. Of the original five dimensions, Power Distance is, to us, the most key,

> "Power Distance... the extent to which the less powerful members of organizations and institutions accept and expect that power is distributed unequally. It suggests that a society's level of inequality is endorsed by the followers as much as by the leaders. ..."[133]

In other words, it is not the power *they take*, but the power *we give* them. That was quite a revelation to me when I first read about it!

The lesson then is that we must learn to not give our power away so readily. Not easily done at a global or national level, probably, but feasible at a local level. And there's nothing more "local" than the workplace.

What happens inside a company can vary quite a bit from the country at large. National biases and norms don't disappear, but they can be modulated with lots of behavior modeling. I've seen this at work at Nearsoft. At a Power Distance score of 81,[134] Mexico is a hierarchical society—but not so inside Nearsoft. Training, behavior modeling, and a supportive culture has helped significantly.

Nearsoft's Orientation program has gone from a "hello" and a handshake, to two weeks, and then six weeks. It's been effective at getting new people to recognize the habits they bring with them and then to start to move away from them and replace them with healthier habits (*e.g.*, speak up, self-direct, and let yourself be seen, rather than sulk and complain in the hallways). This Orientation gives a taste of what working at Nearsoft is like, but the transformation is not immediate.

There is a lot to unlearn. According to Pablo Aretxabala, a member of K2K Emocionando, getting starting on the path of co-management takes a couple of months, but "to consolidate the new mindset, behavior, and habits may take two or three years."[135]

Self-Emancipation

Whenever the topic of co-ownership and co-management comes up, the next question is "how can I do it?" And the answer is that creating or transforming into a RADICAL company is going to be difficult. Very exciting and hugely beneficial, but not a walk in the park for either startups or established businesses.

There is a whole ecosystem of consultants who can help you convert to co-management. And there are many companies that are experimenting with aspects it, including Liqueed and Happyforce in Spain, 10Pines, Basetis, and Manas in Argentina, UruIt in Uruguay, Pressto in Peru, Tegu in Honduras, Grupo Cygnus in Chile, and Vagas and Grupo Anga in Brazil, Semillas del Caribe, Grupo Qualia, Zero Transportation in Mexico,[136] and VkusVill in Russia.[137]

Since 2007, K2K Emocionando in Spain has made a business out of helping FIAT businesses convert to co-management, including some aspects of co-ownership. Before they commit to taking on a client, the business owners have to unanimously sign an agreement to keep their hands-off operations and share the company's numbers with the workers. The owners and the workers agree to share profits and risks, but it is not quite co-ownership because the equity remains in the hands of the FIAT owners (*e.g.*, they can sell the company at any time). Nevertheless, K2K has shown that there is a repeatable process to transform established FIAT business into near-RADICAL companies.

As people practice co-management and deconstruct the FIAT house of cards, they also peel off the internal FIAT shackles that we all carry around with us. As this happens and people learn to identify bottlenecks, centralized ownership will stick out like a sore thumb and people will have the skills to do something about it. Nevertheless, converting to co-ownership is going to be a huge hump to get over that only the most daring will attempt. Besides W L Gore in the US, BuurtzorgT in The Netherlands is moving in that direction.

Crisis as Opportunity

Established businesses are more likely to try anything at a time of crisis, even a transformation to co-management. That was the case at SEMCO, a crisis that almost brought them to the point of bankruptcy and also caused its owner, Ricardo Semler, to get their seminal transformation started. As he wrote in Maverick, the transformation helped them get out from under the crisis.

Similarly, at Yash Papers, in India, there was a crisis that kicked off the company's transformation.[138] In 1999, a curfew kept the bosses from getting to the factory, so the workers self-organized, got supplies on credit, and had a record production. The founder, KK Jhunjhunwala, had read Semler's Maverick and he was all for experimenting with co-management. When he passed away, his son, Ved Krishna, kept it up when he took over the company. In 2012, Ved had his own crisis with Yash and also at a personal level. He didn't waste this combined crisis, either. He came up with a new, Earth-friendly product line and doubled down on co-management.

By the way, what happened at Yash shows that co-management can work anywhere in the world. Even, "in a culture where hierarchy is very strongly ingrained."[139] With the help of consultants Pradeep Chakravarthy[140] and Suresh Pandit,[141] they reached back to India's roots and its temple system, when self-governance was alive and well in India. They've adapted these practices to work at Yash and they are well out from under the crisis.

A crisis is an opportunity to get started on the RADICAL journey. The combination of co-management and co-ownership can help a company's financial performance by increasing profits, reducing costs (*e.g.*, turnover). The tradeoff is accepting a loss of the perception of control, but a company in crisis is obviously not under control. If there's one thing that FIAT owners understand is that getting something for nothing is *good* and if it leads out of the crisis, it's even *better*.

13
PEOPLE AT THE CENTER

People as Resources

FIAT businesses don't prioritize people. At all. For FIAT businesses, power and the perception of control are most important. So are the rules. And so are the deadlines, as arbitrary as they might be. And, oh, yeah, be nice.

When Nearsoft was a small company of less than 10 people it was easy enough to prioritize people and put them at the center. Indeed, most startups are people-centered when the team is small and they are aligned to a common vision. Then capital investment happens and all that goes down the FIAT drain and capital takes the top spot. Our revenue is below target? Fire enough *resources* to bring back our. Office rent is going up? Pack *resources* closer together (but leave the corner offices untouched).

But as Angel investor Dr Alicia Castillo would say, "humans are not resources." People are living, breathing social animals, evolved to work with one another. Our work has to make sense to us and we need to know, "why do we have to do *X* instead of *Y*?" We need to understand to contribute, "maybe we should be working on *Z*?" The desire to be part of a group is literally built into our DNA, but it has to be a compatible, aligned group.

None of this was clear to us as we built Nearsoft, it just felt right to put people at the center. By doing what was right for people we created the conditions for what became a people-centered culture, with less of the fear that is so ingrained in FIAT businesses. We treated each other as adults, not as "clients" or "employees," and this created value for us and our clients from day one.

Focusing on people and treating each other as adults was an early expression of where Nearsoft was headed. And it is still serving us well.

Bound by Iron Bars

"Our bureaucratic rules ultimately confine us as solidly as if we were in a cage bound by iron bars."
—*James Barker, Tightening the Iron Cage*[142]

Control is embodied in FIAT bureaucracies. Arbitrary as they may be, bureaucratic rules can be more effective than an armed guard. We just have to follow the rules and we are all treated by the same rules. Richard Edwards, an economist, sees them as a form of tyranny, "… the great contradiction in bureaucratic control is its implicit tyranny. Workers are treated fairly within the rules, but *they have no say in establishing the rules.*[143] These rules become our invisible iron cage.

Professor Gary Hamel and coauthor Michele Zanini wrote a whole book on bureaucracy and they came to the conclusion that we need an alternative, "bureaucracy was invented by human beings and now it's up to us to invent something better."[144] Except every one of our habits keep us from breaking out of the iron cage and reaching out for "something better." Left to their old habits, there's a good chance that a team becomes its worst boss and becomes emotionally attached to its rules and then coerces members to adapt to these rules. This is what professor James Barker calls *concertive control.*

One possible way to avoid this kind of iron cage is to review the team's rules and norms on a regular basis. For example, when a new person joins the team, write down the team's rules and norms individually on pieces of paper and then drop them all in the trash can. Now you have a clean slate! Then, take each rule out of the trash, one at time, and review it. Each rule either earns its place back on the slate or it stays in the trash. Even if new members don't ask any challenging questions (*e.g.,* because they won't yet feel safe enough), the exercise of questioning their own rules *shows* the new folks that 1) we are not attached to the rules we made up in the past, and 2) we have a new team with you in it and we may need new rules.

Structures, Agreements, and Norms

"… conservatives believe that people need external structures or constraints in order to behave well, cooperate, and thrive."

—*Jonathan Haidt, The Righteous Mind*[145]

RADICAL companies are based on structures, agreements, and norms, just like FIAT businesses. The *fundamental* difference is that these structures, agreements, and norms are created by the very people affected by them, not created externally nor handed down by imperial bosses. They are dynamic and adapt to emerging conditions and help the group "behave well, cooperate, and thrive" more effectively than arbitrary orders from on high.

Be careful that regardless of where these structures, agreements, and norms come from, if they stop changing and become immutable, they become a bureaucracy that limits you, limits your ability to cooperate, and prevents you from thriving.

A Joyful Place

> "If people are laughing, they are learning. True learning is a joy because it is an act of creation."
> —*Tyson Yunkaporta, Sand Talk*[146]

Never forget that this is all about people. Companies are but a group of people who are aligned and experiment together and they get joy from the journey.

Richard Sheridan, a friend, entrepreneur, and author of Joy, Inc, is not shy about saying that he co-founded Menlo Innovations, a co-managed company, for "selfish" reasons. "I desperately wanted to work in a joyful place with joyful people achieving joyful outcomes. I wanted to have fun at work while producing wonderful results within a sustainable business."[147] We very much recognize wanting to create a joyful place to do work we love, a place of "… affective relations, sensuality, playing, laughing, loving."[148]

One of the big advantages of *not* having a FIAT hierarchy is that you can make it about what's good and healthy for people as Richard and his co-workers did. Yes, a company has to be sustainable and generate profits, but don't let an obsession with arbitrary financial targets take precedence over people's joy.

Beware that these targets may not look arbitrary and may be positioned as "crushing the competition" or "winning a lucrative deal." Regardless of what the narrative is, you can recognize these decisions when they, 1) are arbitrary, 2) focused on financial targets only, 3) are made by a handful of owners, and 4) dehumanize the workplace.

Whatever you do, a company should be a source of joy. A space where people can bring their whole selves to work, warts and all. This is about making work just another aspect of one's life, no just a miserable survival mechanism.

14
THE FUTURE
OF WORK (AND
EVERYTHING)

Making an Impact

Our existing businesses are broken because FIAT organizations prioritize control and obedience over everything else. You have likely seen the data from Gallup,[149] ADP,[150] and others. The results speak for themselves: most people are disengaged. They're miserable, or numb, or somewhere in between. We think it's time to flip the script and view our organizations through a people lens rather than a simplistic financial one.

Imagine a truly people-centric culture, a workplace where people are valued and have a strong sense of belonging, where they are surrounded by people that encourage each other to find meaning in their work and in all they do. And where there are no bosses to prevent any of this from happening, demanding "more, more." This world has already sparked the imagination of many who are working on making it happen.

Just look at all the different approaches to the so-called Future of Work out there, with more popping up every day. They are all valid reactions to a singular problem: our businesses are broken and they break people.

Doug Kirkpatrick has been a co-management practitioner for a very long time. He was part of the team that kicked off The Morning Star Company. He is also an author[151] and the closest thing to a philosopher of the co-management space. Trying to keep track of the field, he created a Periodic Table[152] of all the different approaches, governance, frameworks, tools, media, associations, networks, conferences, and technologies. He even included what he calls *poets laureate* of the Future of Work, including Dee Hock, Peter Koestenbaum, Peter Drucker, Edgar Schein, Tom Peters, Gary Hamel, Fernando Flores, David Whyte, and Pim de Morree and Joost Minnaar (to which we would add Mary Parker Follet, and Ricardo Semler).

The problem is that our businesses continue to be broken and tactical solutions are not making a significant dent. Economist Umair Haque captures the feeling: "Try as we might to embrace ethics, toe the line of responsibility, and accept fuzzy, vague notions of good citizenship, they seem ever in conflict with the sharp, cold edge of business."[153]

Changing the System

A whole Future of Work industry has emerged. Books, blogs, podcasts, videos, courses, certifications, as well as experts, consultants, and self-proclaimed gurus. You can be happy, have fun at work. You can empower your people. You can learn about the five, eight, or 20 myths about self-management and how to make self-management work in five easy steps.

Some come as packaged solutions, but that doesn't work. As professor, consultant, and author Gary Hamel puts it, "I don't think that there's a single model that's even close to a one-size-fits all."[154] It sounds appealing, really, to have a ready-made recipe, but the right co-management formulation for any group of people can emerge only from experimentation by the people who are going to live it.

The good news is that this reflects a broad hunger for alternatives to FIAT management. A good example of this is the popularity of the book *Reinventing Organizations* written by consultant Frederic Laloux. "Evolutionary Teal" is his label for organizations that fully support the autonomy of its members. According to Laloux, "Teal" is not a destination, "I suggest that leaders don't try to engage their organization saying 'we'll become a Teal organization'."[155] Regardless, people have been inspired by the concept, want to see more of it in practice, and so there is a fledgling organic movement behind it now.

None of these approaches deal with what we consider the fundamental problem: ownership.[156] And the problem, as we see it, is that we can't "fix" the FIAT system by tweaking it while leaving FIAT ownership, its foundations, in place. Both make up a system and the system has to change. "Changing the system might be even less work than pouring water on today's tactical emergency."[157]

PART THREE
OUR RADICAL
COMPANY

15
ALL TOGETHER NOW

WE WANT TO see a world where people matter and are at the center of everything we do. To us, that's worth putting energy into. It's your turn now. Go find others who are crazy enough to embark on this RADICAL journey with you. There are going to be a thousand things to do. This means that you will have to get good at running a thousand experiments at once.

The temptation is going to be there to fall back on FIAT habits. In fact, you will fall back on those habits and won't even notice because that's what you know. The challenge is to develop the sensitivity to recognize when you are drifting back to FIAT habits and to bring forth the courage to experiment with an "unproven," people centered process.

Below are a few practices to help you get started, but be ready to experiment and replace them with whatever works best for you.

On Your Marks...

Let's start a shiny, brand new, RADICAL company!

I had a great idea in the shower this morning, but... wait... what kind of Impact is our new company going to have in the world? What would we be doing this for? And why would anybody want to do this with us, what is our Purpose?

Our RADICAL company is going to be rooted in our need to do things that mean something. *Meaning* and *belonging* aren't just words, they reflect how we engage with one another. We have to create a meaningful space for others to engage and contribute in a way that makes sense to us all and gives us an identity as a group.

Ready, Set, *GO!*

Our RADICAL company is going to be co-owned and co-managed from the get-go, of course. That doesn't mean that I'll ignore the experience I've gained at Nearsoft all these years and we'll have to put up with Jose's and Adrian's suggestions. But we will not impose our "best practices" on our new company. We'll try to tone it down, but it is going to be difficult for us to hold back because the "best practices" habit is hard to shake.

Obviously, our new company won't have an imposed hierarchy or bosses with grandiose titles. But that doesn't mean that we won't have a way to align with each other and form a coherent team. In FIAT organizations, the boss determines what alignment there is to be had. Directly or indirectly, he sets the direction, the goals, assignments, deadlines, and also decides what tools and vendors to use. In a RADICAL organization, you and I and every other contributor will be responsible for defining all that.

To belong in a group is to be aligned with it. Without alignment we are either isolated or simply going along with the group.[158] Full, warm participation in a caring group starts with being aligned. Teams don't have to hug and kiss all the time to function, but they do have to develop affection for each other and appreciation for each other's contributions. If you are chronically just putting up with somebody in your group because you have to, then you two are not really a team.

So, let's leverage our principles, commitments, and practices to create our company.

The RADICAL Kitchen

Our new company would look more like an experimental kitchen, always cooking up new recipes, always making messes, and cleaning up better than before. There's no recipe that works in every instance and we are always trying new, better ones.

What worked for Nearsoft 10 years ago would not work today's Nearsoft and vice versa. In 2007, we were eight people at Nearsoft. As of this writing, we are just well over 450 people and growing. We have no idea what will work for us next year and beyond.

> "*Caminante, no hay camino*
> *Se hace camino al andar.*"
> — Antonio Machafp

> "Wanderer, there is no path,
> You make the path as you walk."

Once we really *get* that we create our own path as we move forward, we'll be well on the way towards creating our own futures,

On your mark	Stand firm on the RADICAL principles (meaning and belonging), commitments (transparency and decentralization), and practices.
Get set	Get your alignment tools ready. Define your company's Impact, Purpose, and Mission (or your version of those).
Go!	Experiment and keep experimenting like it's never going to end (because it's not).

16
TO EACH THEIR OWN

THE BASIC ASSUMPTION of co-ownership is that a company's value is forever changing. As its revenue goes up or down, its value changes. Every time somebody joins or leaves, its value changes, too. Customers come and customers go and every time that happens, its value changes. And as its value changes, so will its ownership.

At the very start, when there's merely a handful of people kicking a company off the ground, a simple, formulaic methodology for assigning ownership may work. But that only works for so long. Later, as the team gets bigger and things get more complex, you'll need a more robust method of distributing and accounting for ownership.

Slicing Pie

As we researched the concept of co-ownership and its related practices, we looked at Slicing Pie.[159] According to Mike Moyer, inventor of Slicing Pie, "the beauty of this thing... is your ability to start working with someone immediately."

Impossible to Figure Out

Moyer is clear that at the start, the value of the company is not "baked." As Moyer points out, trying to guess the value of a new company is a losing proposition. "We don't know how much we're worth. We know that it's impossible to figure out this number, yet people try to do it all the time."[160] Slicing Pie works until capital investors get involved and force a "valuation."

Valuations are a combination of fantasy and desperation. The investor supplies the fantasy, "I'll give you $1M for 25% of the company." By waving its magic wand, the investor has now declared that your company is worth $4M dollars! The desperation is supplied by the entrepreneur: if she thinks that the investors offer is too low but she's desperate enough for a capital infusion, then she'll take it, she'll buy into the fantasy.

But how does anybody know what the company is going to be worth in the future? What if the company grows to $1B in revenue? Does the fellow who invested $1M still owns 25% of the company no matter how large it gets? And, what about the people who did the work to turn the $1M into a $1B, what about the so-called employees? "Well, they got paid, didn't they?"

The value of a company is also "impossible to figure out" even after capital investors get involved. In the co-ownership model the pie never "bakes."

The Pie Keeps Growing

As Moyer points out, The Slicing Pie rules are aimed at small, pre-investment teams. During a lecture at Stanford, Moyer said that, "when you go to your VC, ... your real money investor ... we're not playing by [the Slicing Pie] rules anymore, we're playing by regular business rules."[161] However, investment capital is no more "real" than the time and creativity invested by the people who make the company happen.

To be clear, a capital infusion can be very valuable. Besides the money itself, it signals that the company has become tangible enough for outsiders to bet on it. The investment is very welcome and celebrated in RADICAL companies, too. However, in the RADICAL case that a *financial* investment does not grant investors any powers beyond a right to a *financial* reward.

In the FIAT model, capital takes over all financial and strategic decisions and relegates everybody to, at best, a financial beneficiary role. Whether they keep the founders around or they bring in their own CEO, the FIAT owners are in charge. The RADICAL ownership model flips this situation on its head: capital is the financial beneficiary and members retain the power to make financial, strategic, and operational decisions. If changes are needed, that's up to the people who embody the company, not to the capital investors.

According to Moyer, "Equity in a startup company is the risk that you are not going to get paid. Equity in an established company... it's more of an incentive, a bonus..."[162] He is describing what is "normal" today in our FIAT world: if you are not taking a capital risk, then you are just acquired labor, a mere employee. We find it mind-blowing that the same people who embrace the idea that ownership is an incentive for them can then turn around and declare that a fixed salary is plenty enough for everybody else. If ownership is a motivator for founders, then why wouldn't it be just as strong a motivator for everyone in the team? "Well, yes, you have to give them some equity, but keep them out making real decisions, they are not owners."

Another way to interpret this approach is that once "real money" makes a bet, all the rest of us have to do is execute according to the plan. Creativity and commitment is no longer important. "We just need people who can take orders and follow the plan." This is the very mindset that is holding back our economies and making us all miserable and disengaged.

On the other hand, the co-ownership approach assumes that the "plan" is never perfect and it takes fully engaged and committed people to make a business thrive and grow. Co-ownership is the giant disrupting force that's going to improve people's well-being and growth and that is going to make our companies thrive financially beyond anything we've seen so far.

Valuing the Intangible

One of the things that Slicing Pie touches upon is how to get the founders and other early people a bigger slice of the pie. Moyer calls that "calibrating" or "partitioning" the pie,

> "... early Grunts can 'harvest' some of the value they have created by calibrating the theoretical value to a higher number. The new value becomes the base against which they (and new Grunts entering the herd) will earn additional pie. Care must be taken to ensure that the new, calibrated amount does not overestimate what the actual value of the company will eventually be. If it does, the Grunts will be unhappy. As an alternative to calibration, the Grunts can 'partition' off part of the pie and split up the rest. Their partitioned percentage remains fixed while the rest changes based on inputs from the herd."[163]

Ignoring the "grunt" and "herd" terminology, what Moyer is talking about is valuing the intangible. What is the original idea for the company worth? What about the many pivots that the founders went through before the company found its market? We can see how people who feel they've made a breakthrough would want to reward themselves. I sure did. This kind of accomplishment is cathartic, an experience that changes everyone involved. The founders' actions need to be recognized in a tangible way, but "calibration" and "partitioning" are ham-fisted suggestions. His mention of "theoretical value" and his advice to "not overestimate what the actual value of the company will eventually be" go against Moyer's own "impossible to figure out" observation.

Elsewhere in this book, we consider different ways to recognize the founders' contribution, including financially (*i.e.*, once there *is* something to divvy up).

17
RADICAL COMPENSATION

COMPENSATION, INCLUDING SALARY, has traditionally been treated as a function of performance. It feels awfully reminiscent of the allowance that some kids get from their parents. "If you don't behave, I won't give you your allowance." But salary is not an allowance or tied to individual performance, salary is a form of wealth extraction. For sure, salary is limited by the performance of the whole business, but trying to pin it on one person is misguided, ineffective, and counterproductive.

Haier, a Chinese business that has become the poster child of self-management lately, has tried several compensation models. Their latest experiment is what they call their Customer Paid Salary System.[164] Although we don't find the approach transformational, it is an attempt at breaking out of the fixed salary model.

An example of disintermediated salaries is Manas, a small Argentinian software development company. On their own, they came up with a scheme very similar to the Rosedale Distribution. Founder Nicolas di Tada explains that, "... the only thing this system does is to compute in a short time the optimal compensation scheme between team members... through a distributed, uniform and disintermediated process."[165]

The first time I heard about self-set salaries was in 2007 while reading Maverick. Currently, several companies are using various forms of decentralized salaries, including BvdV, Finext, Hanno, Incentro, Makers Academy, The Morning Star, Smarkets,[166] Ragnarson,[167] Liqueed, Happyforce, 10Pines, Basetis, and Manas.[168] Unfortunately, at Nearsoft we got stuck in the FIAT way of assigning salaries and have not made any serious experiments to change this.

Different types of wealth extraction, including salaries, can be practiced at the same time. There doesn't have to be a one-and-only way of doing it—that is FIAT thinking. You'll need to experiment with different approaches.

Below are a handful of ideas to get you started, but there many other alternatives around this topic and we hope that more will come up.

The Salary Offer

How can we determine a starting salary for new people? This is pretty difficult to do fairly, actually.

The FIAT way is pretty straightforward. Tell me how much you made at your previous job and I'll offer a bit more, but not too much. We can make up the difference with a bigger title, OK? But people have learned to evade talking about their previous salaries and they talk about what they want instead. Either way, you ask and I counter-offer.

A supposedly more progressive way to do this is for you to write down your number and for the employer to write his number. You disclose your numbers to each other and if the employer's offer is the same or higher than your ask, then you join, otherwise you pass. Either way, this still places two people competing across a table. And this kind of competition leaves a bad aftertaste.

In the RADICAL case, once we are ready to invite her to join, let her figure out a salary that works for her and the company. She already is a de facto member and with the help of other members, she can identify people who are most like her. Those people can even suggest others who would be even more akin to her in skills, experience, etc. She could then get together with her peers and figure out a starting salary for her.

This can actually go much faster than the traditional FIAT way. The right people get involved from the beginning and get to know each other, build trust, and figure out this puzzle together. No negotiation necessary and no bad aftertaste.

Predictable Recurring Income

When you really think about it, "salary" is a FIAT tool. Employees get income predictability in exchange for obedience, follow orders and get a paycheck. Salaries, such as they are today, do not quite fit in the RADICAL context. In fact, the subject first came up as we were writing this book, I thought messing with salaries was wrong-headed. After a lot of back and forth, this is what we came up with,

- Each member determines their Predictable Recurring Income (PRI). This is what they need to take home every month. Some people will start too high and others will start too low, but we will all learn over time.

- For the company, along with expenses, loan repayment, and other fixed expenses, the sum of all PRIs determines what for simplicity we'll call the company's *breakeven point*.

- Every month, the company pays its bills and all PRIs and what's left is distributed as Earned Dividends according to each person's RAD allocations. This is the happy path.

- When revenue doesn't cover the breakeven point, a PRI Account for each member provides predictability. As a company we take on a debt obligation in exchange for an investment into this fund. Then, as needed, money flows out of the PRI Account to cover a member's full PRI.

- Each co-owner is responsible for her PRI Account and has to pay back what they got out of it. Most likely, this will be paid back out of Earned Dividends once revenue goes above breakeven, but this is something you'd have to experiment with.

- In the worst case, if the company goes belly up, then if the PRI Account was funded with investment money, there's no "debt" to be paid back. If it was funded with a loan, then people with unpaid balances have to make good on that loan.

For a more detailed explanation and examples of what this may look like, see Wealth Extraction.

This is one way of dealing with the RADICAL equivalent of salaries, experiment and figure out what works for you.

Not Just for Startups

Something like the PRI scheme is not limited to new companies. It would also work when an organization is faced with a financial crisis. When revenue plummets, some co-owners will be able to handle it financially, and some won't. Their declared PRIs tell which is which.

It would also work for individual situations, when co-owners go through major, unexpected changes in their lives. Just imagine the surprise of having quintuplets—that would change anybody's PRI, big time. The five-times parent could raise her PRI, at least for a while.

There is also the not-so-happy situation where a company cannot sustain its PRI. Members are drawing most or all of their PRI from their Accounts and there's little chance that the company can ever reach breakeven. In that case, the team may have to revisit the PRI levels and do something about the situation.

Whatever the case, PRIs are not a magic wand to wish away hard times or difficult decisions.

The PRI scheme is transparent and decentralized. It affords everybody more agency, makes dealing with hard times a lot less stressful, and can lead to better decisions. Also, the fact that it gives everybody a chance to learn to handle risk will make our companies, and our economies, more resilient.

18
SPLITTING THE ATOM

AT FIRST WE thought that this section's title was a bit too dramatic, but splitting power from capital may be a lot more difficult than splitting the atom. The idea that power and capital are one thing is pretty old, and many FIAT owners are going to feel that co-ownership robs them of... something. And it does, it robs them of governance power, though not of their money nor their participation and ability to contribute.

On the other hand, separating power from capital is what the financial markets already do: when you buy common stock in the stock markets you don't get any form of operational or strategic control. None. You bought the stock on the bet that you can later sell it at a higher price. In the meantime, you have no say in how the business is run, who is in charge, or what the company's market strategy should be. So long as its stock price is going up, you are supposed to be as happy as a pig in mud. If something bothers you about the business, your only practical option is to sell its stock at the best price you can get.

Rather than power, as an investor in a RADICAL company you get a predictable financial return. And it does not prevent you from contributing to the company in other ways, becoming a co-owner of it, and earning a voice in its direction.

FIAT Ownership

Traditional ownership is about having control over a business. In FIAT owned businesses the Board of Directors[169] is the top owner. Directors are supposed to be fiduciaries who act "in the interest of" all shareholders. Among other things, the Board is responsible for,

- Attesting the business' performance to other shareholders.
- Broad governance policies.
- Making sure there's enough financing to meet goals.
- Approving annual budgets.
- Setting compensation for execs, the top bosses.
- How much to pay as dividends, if any.
- Ownership distribution (*e.g.*, options and stock grants).
- Fate of the company (*e.g.*, selling all or part of it).

They must do "the right things" or risk getting booted out or sued by the rest of the shareholders. And doing "the right things" boils down to making sure the business is *financially profitable.* Everything else is secondary, including the impact of decisions on employees.

Real Contributions

In the FIAT model investors get "a seat on the Board" or some other form of power over operations. When a RADICAL company accepts a capital infusion, it takes on a financial obligation but it doesn't assign it any other special powers,

- Capital does not automatically force a valuation.
- Ownership continues to be dynamically allocated by the co-owners as the company grows.
- Capital does not beget operational power. In particular, it does not include the power to arbitrarily hire and fire. Although in theory a Board doesn't have operational control, in practice it has the power to fire the CEO which gives it a huge influence over operations.

In reality, when a company is heading off the rails, the people who show up to work every day will know about it well before a traditional Board even hears about it. In a FIAT company that information will eventually get to the Board, emphasis on eventually. Co-owners of a RADICAL company are more likely to move to fix this situation earlier, more decisively, and in a more nuanced way than a traditional Board. *Their* business is at stake, and more importantly, *their* impact, *their* purpose, and *their* mission are at risk. *Their lives* are on the line. They are in a better position to pass judgement, make the right decision, and find a healthy way to address it.

There is nothing preventing a RADICAL investor from becoming part of the team, too. But she would not carry any more weight than any of her co-owners. It may be that an investor has the best, most balanced suggestions and people follow it. Her experience, not the girth of her investment, leads the way and the company benefits from it. Our RADICAL investors can lead because of the value of her contributions, not her capital.

Utterly Ridiculous

Another reason why splitting power from capital is going to be difficult is because this whole RADICAL thing will sound foreign to many people, not just FIAT owners. For example,

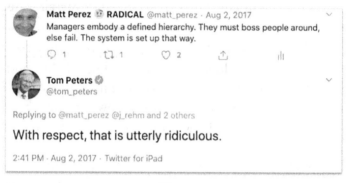

Matt Perez ⬛ RADICAL @matt_perez · Aug 2, 2017 ⌄
Managers embody a defined hierarchy. They must boss people around, else fail. The system is set up that way.

🗨 1   ↻ 1   ♡ 2   ⬆   ılı

Tom Peters ✓
@tom_peters   ⌄

Replying to @matt_perez @j_rehm and 2 others

With respect, that is utterly ridiculous.

2:41 PM · Aug 2, 2017 · Twitter for iPad

170

Peters has consistently and enthusiastically celebrated the "excellence" that people are capable of bringing to the table. Where we part ways with Peters is in putting the burden completely on the individual when the problem really is with the way businesses operate. It's the barrel, not the apples. Individual heroics will always run up against what's allowed by the FIAT system most businesses operate under. By all means, individuals should aim for excellence and heed the direction that Peters points to. But they don't have a chance to make a lasting impact unless we create companies where *everybody* can pursue excellence, not just "managers."

Understandably, it is difficult to conceive of any other way of organizing a company other than the FIAT way. The same way that most people on July 3, 1776 could not conceive of any other way of running a country without a King. And even after the US declared independence from George III, many Europeans, particularly the British, and more than a few Americans continued to question how soon it was going to take before the American experiment would collapse.

Back then, nobody knew for certain if it would work, but most of the experiments leading up to it pointed to "yes." The 13 American Colonies had been experimenting quite a bit with different flavors of governance. And the experimenting has never stopped.

Unfortunately, the "you need a strong hand" feeling has persisted. Even in the late 1960s, I had a very dear family member who believed that Generalísimo Franco was good for Spain. "This country needs a strong man to lead it to prosperity." Never mind that Franco was a dictator and had an authoritarian choke on Spain, very much like the one we had left behind in Cuba.

The French Revolution and its quick retreat to Napoleon's authoritarian rule gave fuel to the "strong hand" camp. Edmund Burke, Thomas Paine's nemesis, bemoaned that "when the old feudal and chivalrous spirit of fealty… shall be extinct in the minds of men, plots and assassinations will be anticipated by preventive murder and preventive confiscation…"[171] It sounds like today's predictions that without a boss there will be chaos and mayhem at work.

Where would employees get their direction from? Are they going to figure this out by themselves? When will they have time to do real work? How else would you make sure that the employees are working hard to make the owner wealthier?

It only follows that any talk of moving away from the FIAT hierarchy cannot not make sense to people who have shaped their lives around the FIAT organization and that management regime. It cannot make sense to people who have moved up the FIAT ladder, one painful rung after another.

As Gary Hamel describes it, "… if you've spend your entire life playing this massive multiplayer game called bureaucracy and learning how to accumulate and use bureaucratic power… when someone tells you, 'now I am going to change the game' is like saying to someone like LeBron James, a basketball player, that now we are going to play volleyball… probably not going to be enthusiastic about that."[172]

For these folks the whole co-management thing cannot be but "utterly ridiculous" (they also are going to be fiercely resistant to co-ownership).

In the Interest of

The "interest of" a RADICAL company includes its financial success, of course. But that is secondary to the success of each of its members, and the success of its customers, partners, providers, and whatever other communities it touches. Financial success, yes, but not as the only metric. The "interest of" a RADICAL company includes providing an opportunity for people to find meaning and purpose in their work and to work with a group they are aligned with and that supports each other.

RADICAL companies are co-owned. It is "in the interest of" these companies that ownership be decentralized and dynamic. That ownership reflects who's contributed to others and therefore to the company. Anything else would definitely not be "in the interest of" a RADICAL company.

RADICAL companies are co-managed. It is in the "interest of" these companies that there'd be no command-and-control structure, no imposed hierarchy, and an unshakeable commitment to become fully transparent and decentralized. Anything else would definitely not be "in the interest of" a RADICAL company.

Lots of Jugglers

It takes a lot of things to go right for a company to be successful. Venture Capital opened the door for more entrepreneurs than the system of bankers and wealthy boys clubs that preceded it. It's time for a new model and co-ownership can produce even more entrepreneurs and a higher rate of financial success to companies.

In a RADICAL company ownership is held by many co-owners, not just a select few. Co-owners directly shape the company's ownership structure, its strategy, its governance, its policies, and its operations. They have the right to fully participate in decision making, from the most trivial to the most strategic. Not everyone *will* participate in every decision, but everybody will have the right to. The Leadership Team practice at Nearsoft shows a decision making practice that works at scale. As always, Experiment and figure out what will work for you.

Instead of depending on one extraordinary juggler, multiple co-owners can juggle many more balls at once. And they can do it with less stress, more grace, a broader perspective, and are more likely to be financially successful in the long run.

Capital Budgeting

Besides external investments, we have to think about internal capital investments and make sure that they don't get any special powers either. Retained Earnings is one such internal capital investment. It is, essentially, a piece of our profits we keep in the bank to pay for next year's basic operations and growth projects. Warren Buffet agrees that Retained Earnings are a good thing and quotes well known economist John Maynard Keynes as saying that, "Well-managed industrial companies do not, as a rule, distribute to the shareholders the whole of their earned profits. ... they retain a part of their profits and put them back into the business."[173]

The more capital kept as Retained Earnings, the less capital there is to distribute as Earned Dividends and this impacts all co-owners. This means that unlike FIAT companies, a RADICAL company cannot just do this without involving co-owners. One way to assure a RADICAL company communicates its plans and their impact to all co-owners is to insist that it returns all or most of its earnings to the co-owners, at least symbolically.[174] Some amount of earnings will continue to be retained, otherwise either the company will stop growing or it would have to borrow money to grow. Nevertheless, this process must be fully transparent and intelligible to co-owners.

Somebody needs to explain why so much went into one pot versus another. Then, every team that is partaking of this capital must let the other co-owners know how they plan to invest it, why they need money-in-the-bank capital instead of a percent of cash flow, and what impact this investment is going to have on the co-owners and the company, as best they know. This would create a ritualized way for all co-owners to pay attention and *really* have a say about the future of the company.

This means that it is in the best interest of the company to have co-owners learn how to read the books (*e.g.*, a la Open Book Management), understand retained earnings, and learn to evaluate future plans and the impact it will have on each of them.

Resist the Voice of Fear

This also implies that, unless human nature changes dramatically overnight, plans would be more or less publicly known. This will be a recurring excuse to not disclose "at least some" of the plans. But keeping "at least some" things behind closed doors is another form of power grabbing. For example, this is the approach that governments take with their "closed doors briefings," but as US Circuit Judge Damon Keith warned, "Democracies die behind closed doors... When government begins closing doors, it selectively controls information rightfully belonging to the people. Selective information is misinformation." The same applies to RADICAL companies.

Resist the voice of fear. The fact that "our competition will know" is an empty scare tactic. Our competition may copy everything you do, but they cannot copy you. For example, Amazon decided in 2000 to switch their servers from Sun Microsystems to HP/Linux. It was one of the worst kept secrets ever, their competitors knew about it, and they didn't copy them. When finished, Amazon's costs dropped dramatically and so did their competitors. Or take the US steel industry who would not copy what the Japanese steel producers were doing to increase their productivity. The price of steel dropped and the biggest US steel makers disappeared. Everything about how Buurtzorg does things is well known and widely published, but others in their industries have not copied them. They are too arrogant to do that.

At Nearsoft we've had a competitor copy many of the things we did, but to no avail. A lot of their "employees" preferred to become Nearsoftians and many have come over to our side of the street. Some of their clients, too, found our culture more attractive and preferable to work with and made the switch.

The other myth is that "our clients would know." But if you have to keep secrets from your clients, then you definitely have a serious problem that you need to resolve first.

19
LIQUIDITY

LIQUIDITY IS A form of autonomy. An ESOP account that holds wealth for me is nice, but it is not liquid like a bank account is. My bank account is liquid, my ESOP account is not.

Getting RADs that represent what we've earned as a company is very nice. But after the excitement of the recognition that comes with them, then what? What can you do with them? Could you buy a car?

I Need a Car

One use case is how to provide liquidity for individuals. Here's one way this could work.

I need cash to buy a car now, so I offer to lease out my RADs' financial yield for a given period. This means that whoever takes me up on it would get the cash I would normally get through my RADs. Say, for example, that I can show that my Earned Dividends are between $3,500 and $4,000 in cash every month (*i.e.*, above my Predictable Recurring Income). In six months I can expect to earn, in total, between $18,000 and $24,000. But I need to buy a car *now* so I *offer to accept* $18,000 for the "lease" of my RADs' yield for six months.

An investor (*i.e.*, anybody inside or outside the company) takes me up on it, gives me $20,000, and I buy a used car. By the end of the six-month period, this could add up to more than 30% gross return for the investor. The return is not an interest that I pay, but comes out of the value that the company creates.

I forgo that extra wealth, but the advantage to me is that the company pays for the yield and I get the car I need sooner. For the investor, this arrangement has advantages, too,

- Because of the short period of time, the Present Value of money is not significant.
- The risk is minor because the time period is shorter and the collateral is the cash generating value of the company.
- This kind of investment would require a lot less due diligence.
- It also requires much less participation by the investor.
- The quick return means that investors could recycle their gains more quickly.

At the end of five months, the investor would have no further rights to any wealth generated by my RADs, regardless of the actual total payout. This is an investment, not a loan, and the risk that the investor takes is that the company may generate less cash than in the past. A capital investment based on expected future performance is a traditional tool of capitalism.

Since this all happens transparently, another investor, say, a co-worker, may "offer to invest" at a lower, more competitive rate (*e.g.*, $18,000 for a *five-month* lease of your RADs). Or a group of co-workers could put up an Investment Club Banner to do these types of investments on a regular basis. Or a RADICAL bank could do these investments very competitively. Or... you get the idea.

The Bull, Inc Exchange

SAIC was a consulting business founded by Dr Robert Beyster in 1969. Dr Beyster wanted to build a business that produced wealth for everyone, not just for him. Over time, Dr Beyster's holdings went "... from 100 percent to 10 percent in the first year of the company's existence, and to less than 2 percent by the 1990s."[175] By the time he exited, the business had grown to $8B in revenue, which made Dr Beyster's 2% worth $160M.

SAIC employees were financial beneficiaries in a big way. Nevertheless, the employees were symbolic owners only because the Board and management remained in control. In the end, the Board forced Dr Beyster out of the business, sold it, and the business has since pretty much disappeared.

To provide liquidity for SAIC employees, as Dr Beyster explains, "... we started up this wholly owned broker-dealer subsidiary dubbed Bull, Inc., to create a limited market in the stock and help facilitate the transfer of stock from employees who desired to sell SAIC stock to buyers," this gave SAIC folks "a mechanism for buying and selling stock while remaining with SAIC."[176] Bull would set the stock price and "any shareholder could offer vested stock for sale in the internal market."[177]

Creating Bull, Inc showed Dr Beyster's commitment to spreading ownership among SAIC's employees. He went further than most to give SAIC employees a financial stake in the business and then created Bull, Inc for liquidity. For a business that was founded in 1969, this is pretty mind blowing.

One might be tempted to think, and we were, that it would be a good idea to create a similar market for RADICAL companies, but we came to the conclusion that it doesn't make sense. RADs represent all aspects of your contribution according to your peers, not just financial value. You might have gotten some of your RADs because you took the time to talk to another co-owner when she was having a particularly bad day. How would you *trade* that?

20
INVESTMENT CAPITAL

BEYOND PROVIDING LIQUIDITY for individuals, we may need to provide investment capital for big company projects. Some of it might come from Retained Earnings, or we could save up for it, or come up with a RAD leasing scheme that would work for capital investors, or we could borrow from a RADICAL bank.

Self-Owned Assets

Revenue, time, and even honorifics could easily be factored through RADs. But what about a building or a fleet of trucks? In a FIAT business, its owner owns the asset. But since ownership is decentralized and dynamic in a RADICAL company, how would it work? Who paid for the building? Who gains from it? One month I may end up with 10% of all the RADs and six months later it may be 3%. If we bought the building when I was at 10%, does that mean that six months later I would own only 3% of it? One way to handle this is to have the building own itself.[178]

Imagine that we at BenCo had agreed to put up a banner that would allow us to accumulate $5M to buy the building in three years. Once we had the money, we would invest it in JerryCo to buy the building and lease it back to BenCo. We are doing this not to obfuscate ownership or avoid taxes, quite the opposite this would make things more transparent and easier to understand and explain.

The percentage ownership of that investment would be determined by the number of RADs each person owns at *the time of the investment.* If I had 10% of all the allocated RADs at that point, I would own 10% of the $5M investment. If six months later my RADs went down to 3% of the total BenCo RADs, I still would own 10% of the investment that we made on JerryCo six months ago. This makes it easy for a member to understand how much of *that* building *she* owns.

Not every member would have to participate in this invest-ment. Some members may not want to or can't participate. Others would participate for a while and then stop, or vice versa. In any case, each month the Banner would get money disbursed to it as a function of its RADs until we have enough to purchase the building.

As part of its "constitution," JerryCo would define how much of its profits to keep for maintenance, taxes, end-of-life, etc., and what to do with the dividends. One possibility is to use all its dividends to pay back the $5M plus a return. (See RADICAL Investment, below). If later on BenCo stops using the building, JerryCo could put it up for lease to another company (and disburse those dividends to the JerryCo co-owners). If later JerryCo wanted to put solar panels on the building, another Banner would go up and the process would repeat.

RAD Leasing

A RADICAL company could lease RADs' yield to a capital investor.

For example, imagine a small company that needs $200,000 to buy Cloud services to get more paying customers. To do this, its co-owners would agree, for example, to have the company retain a percentage of RADs to lease to an investor.

An investor puts money up front, in exchange for rights to the RADs' yield, the company uses the money to get the Cloud services it needs, it gets more paying customers, redeems the RADs as per the terms of the agreement.

As always, experiment.

RADICAL Investment

A RADICAL investment is much like an investment from a VC. The company gets a cash infusion to create new products or expand into new markets. The significant difference is that a RADICAL investment is a purely financial transaction and includes no other rights.

The investment terms will include a risk multiplier and a timeframe and amount for repayment. This could be something like, "we will pay back three times the amount in three years hence," or "we will pay back four times the principal amount in two years starting three years from now," or even "we will pay back three times the amount if we reach X level of revenue, five times if we get to Y level of revenue, and ten times if our revenue grows beyond Z"). Again, the investor does not get any other rights.

Specifically, a RADICAL investor doesn't get company stock, she doesn't get seat on the mythical Board, she doesn't get to "fire the CEO," she doesn't get to demand that the company change directions, and she doesn't get to sell the company because "revenue is not where it should be." We would hope that the investor brings with her something other than money. If that's the case, the investor may be a valuable advisor and mentor and may be invited to discussions where her expertise and informed opinion are key. She may even get RADs for significant contributions. But this is all up to the co-owners and not a given part of the investment. Company governance remains with the co-owners, not the financial investors.

Like any investment, a RADICAL investment comes with the risk that things won't work out and it will not be repaid. So why do RADICAL investments at all?

Every co-owner wants their business to succeed and they want to turn the investment into a blow out financial success. Their self-interest is perfectly aligned with the financial investor's interest.

If problems arise, co-owners will be the first to recognize them. Other co-owners will know right away and in an unfiltered way (i.e., transparency).

Co-owners have the wherewithal to come up with solutions or ways around a problem.

There is very little chance of, say, a founder taking the company in the wrong direction for long without other co-owners noticing, voicing it, and doing something about it.

Overall, a RADICAL investment is less risky than the traditional risk capital investment because everyone in the company, and not just a select few, is committed to its success and fully supportive of it.

A RADICAL Bank

Since 2007 K2K Emocionando,[179] a consulting firm in Northern Spain, has helped many companies transform from FIAT management to co-management. These companies have come together as the NER Group.[180]

In 2009, the NER Group created a bank. Commercial banks were often of no help to the NER Group companies even though these banks were making plenty of money off them. When they did help, their services were expensive in spite of the fact that the NER Group companies had impeccable credit records. This became a problem during the 2010 financial crisis. In response the NER Group companies created Kutxa NER,[181] a non-profit bank capitalized by the NER companies with a small percentage of their annual revenue.

Similarly, a RADICAL bank would likely better serve the needs of RADICAL companies funded by RADICAL companies. Among other services, it would provide credit to these companies when needed. Perhaps, if there had been a RADICAL Bank around, the co-owners of New Belgium Brewery would have not sold the company to Kirin. They might have voted against the acquisition if they had the capital to expand to internatioanl markets.

To be clear, this is not meant to stop RADICAL companies from failing. The bank is meant to increase their staying power and provide them with options. Ultimately, we want to see a steady increase in the number of RADICAL companies. We want the RADICAL paradigm to become the norm and with platforms like RADICAL banks in place, it would be more likely for this to happen.

21
INACTIVE MEMBERS

You Can Take It with You

INACTIVE MEMBERS GET to keep their RADs. However, the number of RADs will increase over time, and the inactive member's RADs will become a smaller percentage of the total RADs. They will continue to get dividends as a factor of their RADs, but as a percentage they will get less and less over time.

For example, imagine that when our member, Anita, goes inactive she has 1,000 RADs or 1% of the 100,000 RADs allocated. If we generate $100,000 in dividends, she gets $1,000 (*i.e.*, bottom left in the graph below). Later, the number of allocated RADs grows to 150,000 total, and dividends to $120,000. Our inactive member still has 1,000 RADs or what is now 0.67% of the total and she gets $800. Later still, the number of allocated RADs grows to 240,000 and dividends to $140,000, so she gets 0.42% of the total or $583.

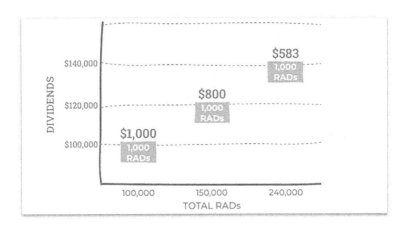

Lucky You

Of course, said inactive member could get lucky.

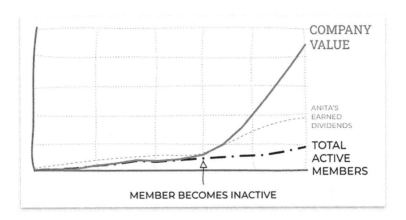

But this is not really luck: she contributed to whatever made the company's value shoot up, so she deserves to benefit financially from her work. Either way, over time Anita's contributions are less significant, her percentage of allocated RADs goes down, and her RADs' yield reflects that.

Alternatively, the dilution of inactive members may be determined by a formula. Take your local pizza parlor or favorite small restaurant. In these cases, it may make more sense to set it up so that the factoring value of RADs of inactive members goes down over time. For example, if active members get $1 as a dividend for every RAD in a given month, an inactive member would get 50¢ after being inactive for 12 months, 25¢ after 24 months, and zero after 36 months.

Cashing Out?

Selling your RADs is not an option. RADs represent your voice in matters of governance and that cannot be sold. At the same time, a member going inactive (*e.g.*, retiring, for so long as that's a thing) may want to get cashed out: she'd prefer cash-in-hand over future value. An option is for the company to retire her RADs in exchange for a predictable monthly payout. We can imagine other alternatives, but, as always, experiment.

Note that this "cashing out" remains a financial transaction. In a FIAT business, owners sell their governance rights along with their financial rights because they are one and the same. In a RADICAL company, the only thing that can be transacted is the rights to the RADs' financial yield, not governance rights.

Who's Inactive?

This brings up the question of who can be considered inactive? Is there a criteria?

"Full-time" and "part-time" are not useful; "on payroll" or not don't make sense, either. We think the only criteria would be based on whether or not a member receives RADs at Distributions. If a member does not receive any RADs for a number of cycles in a row, then she could be considered inactive. Retiring or quitting members will lose their governance rights this way. But even somebody who works every day could lose his governance rights if he has not made any contributions (*i.e.*, received no RADs) for a while. On the other hand, somebody who contributes once a month and gets RADs for it would be considered an active member.

As always the answer is that there is no right answer and you'll have to experiment to find out who is considered inactive in your case.

22
COMING UP NEXT...

Outgoing: FIAT

THE FIAT DOGMA goes something like this: There is, and alway has been, a hierarchy of power that rules every aspect of our being, our society, and our world. Without it, we'd be nothing but wild beasts. Men rule over women, adults rule over children, the armed rule over the defenseless, the powerful rules over the weak, and the gods rule over us all. Our superiors order us about as they see fit, and we happily obey; then we do the same to our subordinates and expect the same obedience.

This mindset is pervasive and invisible, like water to the proverbial fish. Every aspect of our world is born of it. "Today's capitalist economic order is a monstrous cosmos, into which the individual is born and which in practice is for him, at least as an individual, simply a given, an immutable shell..., in which he is obliged to live."[182] This is what German sociologist Max Weber wrote in 1905, more than 100 years ago.

This immutable cage, is slowly imploding and will crush us unless we find alternatives.

Before Copernicus, the dogma of the time had planet Earth at the center of the known Universe. Copernicus moved the Sun to the center instead, set Earth rotating around it, and opened our eyes to an expanding Universe. According to the FIAT dogma, capital, ownership, and power are fused together. He who has the capital is the owner and has the ultimate power. Breaking apart capital, ownership, and power is going to be harder than moving the Sun and Earth, but we'll have to do it to survive. We need a different paradigm, one that puts all of us at the center and lets us all thrive.

Emerging: RADICAL

People are *co-owners* of the company and expect to know about and have a say on major ownership decisions that affect them. This applies to strategic decisions with any impact on the people who embody the company.

People are capable of *co-managing* to get things done because they have the skills to do it. That's what they learned at home and school. They've heard stories of bosses and such, but those feel like tales from a cheap dystopian novel.

People are sensitive to any obstacle that gets in the way of doing *meaningful* work, the voice to point them out, the imagination to find ways around them, and the group skills to remove them.

People join teams because they feel aligned with their explicit impact and purpose. They know they can contribute to the team's mission and want to be part of it, want to *belong* to it. They have learned to "tell their truths, take responsibility, and accept accountability,"[183] individually and as teams.

People have the sensitivity to see when *transparency* or *decentralization* are being blocked. They are committed to removing these blocks so that we can continue to make progress.

People have the confidence to experiment and the capacity to learn from the results. They have learned to come together and work towards an explicit Purpose to make an Impact on the world.

Make It the Norm

We want the RADICAL paradigm to become the norm. We want to see co-owned and co-managed companies become the norm, places where people come to work together and share the result of their effort equitably. The training grounds for people to craft their own paths, make collaboration a habit, and own their destinies. What people learn at *their* companies will then spread to our homes, our schools, our communities, and eventually to a world "more natural, organic, yet maybe evolutionary."[184]

Human nature resists the unknown, and the suggestions in this book will be seen as suspicious at best.

We hope that this book has helped give shape to an "insight which was already yours."[185]

*Change is possible
because it is necessary*

— *John Zerzan* [186]

APPENDICES

1
RADICAL PARADIGM SUMMARY

A Three Legged Stool

HERE'S HOW WE see the foundations of a RADICAL company,

Principles	Meaning and Belonging
Commitments	Transparency and Decentralization
Practices	Alignment and Experimentation

Alignment

Alignment must be explicit.

We think of it as the company's *what for*, its *why*, and its *what, how,* and *when*; we call these Impact, Purpose, and Mission, respectively. However you express them, they have to be explicit and accessible to everyone.

RADICAL Distribution

Instead of cash or stocks, RADICAL Distribution uses a dimensionless unit we call a RAD. RADs account for the unaccountable and can be allocated for anything that contributes to our common effort. Later, RADs can be used to factor any kind of contribution, not just financial.

We may do allocation daily or at whatever rate works for you and combine that with a monthly Distribution celebration.

Banners

Distribution Banners can stand for teams, special accomplishments, new products, community projects, scholarships, etc.

Retrospectives

In a RADICAL Retrospectives members discuss the criteria they used to allocate RADs. Participation in these Retrospectives is voluntary and members can share as much as they'd like of their criteria. These do not prevent people from making their own decisions, but it serves as a guide.

They could be held, for example, after monthly Distribution celebrations.

Feedback

Anybody who wants to can call for a feedback session after a Distribution. In particular, people who didn't get anything or significantly less than they expected would want to do this. Better than letting it fester.

It might be difficult to hear the feedback, but it's the way to grow. It can help resolve latent tensions, correct wrong impressions, and get better results in the future.

For more, see RADICAL Distribution.

Wealth Extraction

You can calculate the amount each co-owner has earned by factoring the total company revenue through the allocated RADs. For example,

- Six of us generate $16,000 in dividends.
- There are a total of 1,000 RADs allocated.
- This means that each RAD factors $16 this cycle.
- You have 450 allocated RADs and I have 130,
- You earned $7,200 and I've earned $2,080 this cycle.

That earned amount is split between a Predictable Recurring Income and Earned Dividend component.

Predictable Recurring Income (PRI)

The PRI is what every co-owner takes home every period (*e.g.*, biweekly or monthly),

- If I earned more than my PRI, then I can take home my PRI and my Earned Dividends.
- If what I've earned matches my PRI, then I take that much home.

- If I earned less than my PRI, I still take home the amount of money I expected, because the PRI Account makes up the difference. But I now owe the difference to this fund.

You'll have to experiment with how these debts are settled. At its loosest, I could pay that debt "later" (e.g., out of my future Earned Dividends). At its most rigid, I'd have to pay the PRI Account debt, plus interest, within 60 days. Go for a policy that matches your current situation. Don't yield to your imagined fears: if a problem crops up, then see if the policy needs to be changed.

In the example below, Salim, Daliah, Alicia, and Anita earned enough dividends to cover their full PRI; Kim and Julio earned less than their PRI, so money flows out of the PRI Account to make up the difference and they, individually, now owe this much to this fund.

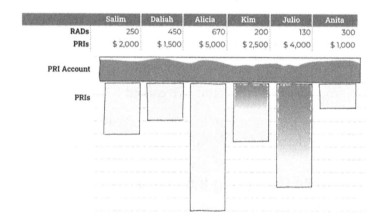

	Salim	Daliah	Alicia	Kim	Julio	Anita
RADs	250	450	670	200	130	300
PRIs	$2,000	$1,500	$5,000	$2,500	$4,000	$1,000

Earned Dividends

Below there are three sample scenarios for how Earned Dividends are calculated,

- Below breakeven: When we as a company don't generate enough Dividends to cover everybody's PRIs in full and the difference has to come out of the PRI Accounts.

- At breakeven: When we make enough to at least pay everybody's PRI.

- Above breakeven: When we as a company can pay everybody's PRI and disburse Earned Dividends.

This first scenario, below breakeven, is what normally happens at the start of a company when it doesn't generate enough revenue to cover everybody's PRI. In this case, we would need an investment or loan to put into the PRI fund so we can use it to meet the amount of PRI each person has set.

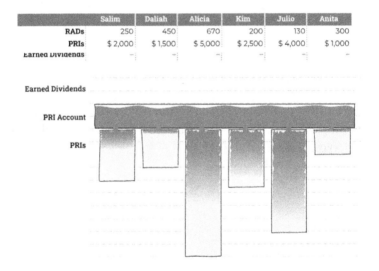

	Salim	Daliah	Alicia	Kim	Julio	Anita
RADs	250	450	670	200	130	300
PRIs	$ 2,000	$ 1,500	$ 5,000	$ 2,500	$ 4,000	$ 1,000
Earned Dividends	–	–	–	–	–	–

In the breakeven case we finally get to pay ourselves fully from the revenue that we've generated. Even in this case, some people may need to draw from the Predictable Recurring Income (PRI) Account, maybe because their PRI are high, or their RADs are low, or both.

	Salim	Daliah	Alicia	Kim	Julio	Anita
RADs	250	450	670	200	130	300
PRIs	$ 2,000	$ 1,500	$ 5,000	$ 2,500	$ 4,000	$ 1,000
DIVIDENDS	$ 16,000 (breakeven)					
Earned	$ 2,000	$ 3,600	$ 5,360	$ 1,600	$ 1,040	$ 2,400
PRI Account	–	–	–	($ 900)	($ 2,960)	–
Earned Dividends	–	$ 2,100	$ 360	–	–	$ 1,600

At some point, after we've been steadily growing our revenue, we start disbursing Earned Dividends in addition to covering everybody's PRI.

	Salim	Daliah	Alicia	Kim	Julio	Anita
RADs	250	450	670	200	130	300
PRIs	$ 2,000	$ 1,500	$ 5,000	$ 2,500	$ 4,000	$ 1,000
DIVIDENDS	$ 25,000 ($ 9,000 above breakeven)					
Earned	$ 3,125	$ 5,625	$ 8,375	$ 2,500	$ 1,625	$ 3,750
PRI Account	--	--	--	--	($ 2,375)	--
Earned Dividends	$ 1,125	$ 4,125	$ 3,375	--	--	$ 2,750

Notice that even though dividends are up, Julio continues to draw from the PRI Account because his PRI is pretty high and his RAD count is pretty low. He may want to change his PRI or get feedback on why his RADs are so low.

2
FROM THE
MANUSCRIPT

THESE APPENDICES WERE at one time or another part of the manuscript but through the various reviews they moved to this section.

On Voting

I own stock in various companies and every so often I get a letter from them to "please, vote" – there's usually a list of names or I can write in a candidate. Every four years we get to vote for our "leaders" in the US. None of it changes the system. Whether you choose chocolate or vanilla, it still is ice cream.

Voting assumes that you choose between rules that apply to everyone. It assumes a monoculture. But life is not a monoculture, it is more subtle than that. I have friends that are gluten intolerant in the US, but they gorge on bread when they go to Europe. I don't want to vote between grain A and grain B, I'd rather partake of breads made with different grains.

It doesn't matter how large or small a company is, groups of people working together are in the best position to figure out what works for them. That's the path to scalability.

In fact, large monolithic organizations are a symptom of the problem that FIAT organizations create, not a shining example to follow.

For example, earlier this afternoon four of us in sales had a conversation about what to do when we have one candidate and many open positions that said candidate could fill. We started the conversation with the assumption that we would come up with a guideline to make these decisions, an eternal rule that will apply in all cases. Instead, we decided that we would have a short meeting with our staffing folks every day and make those kinds of decisions. That's scalable, the original approach was not.

Theory X, Theory Y

In 1957 Professor Douglas McGregor wrote *The Human Side of Enterprise* where he formulated what became known as the Theory X and Theory Y of management. In it, he draws a contrast between the assumptions behind the FIAT belief system (Theory X) versus what he felt were the "proper conditions" to unleash "unimagined resources of creative human energy"[187] (Theory Y).

I suspect that Professor McGregor would not disagree with economist Umair Haque that the world economy is not performing as well as it could[188] and it would perform much better if we really deprecated Theory X altogether.

Theory X	Theory Y
Management is responsible for organizing the elements of productive enterprise—money, materials, equipment, people—in the interest of economic ends.	Management is responsible for organizing the elements of productive enterprise–money, materials, equipment, people–in the interest of economic ends.
With respect to people, this is a process of directing their efforts, motivating them, controlling their actions, modifying their behavior to fit the needs of the organization.	People are not by nature passive or resistant to organizational needs. They have become so as a result of experience in organizations.
Without this active intervention by management, people would be passive—even resistant—to organizational needs. They must therefore be persuaded, rewarded, punished, controlled—their activities must be directed. This is management's task—in managing subordinate managers or workers. We often sum it up by saying that management consists of getting things done through other people.	The motivation, the potential for development, the capacity for assuming responsibility, the readiness to direct behavior toward organizational goals are all present in people. Management does not put them there. It is a responsibility of management to make it possible for people to recognize and develop these human characteristics for themselves. The essential task of management is to arrange organizational conditions and methods of operation so that people can achieve their own goals best by directing their own efforts toward organizational objectives.

Built into Theory X are "several additional beliefs—less explicit, but widespread,"

- The average man is by nature indolent—he works as little as possible.
- He lacks ambition, dislikes responsibility, prefers to be led.
- He is inherently self-centered, indifferent to organizational needs.
- He is by nature resistant to change.
- He is gullible, not very bright, the ready dupe of the charlatan and the demagogue.

Theory X is as widespread today as it's ever been. Whenever you hear people talking about commissions, stake in the outcome, and other money-as-motivator schemes, you are hearing Theory X-speak.

Recruiting

At Nearsoft, a recruiter finds a candidate, tech people with the right skills interview them, and together they make the decision to hire or not. They know best what they need and whether the candidate is qualified. If the new person is not working out, it is the team who is in the best position to figure it out and deal with it.

It seems insane to me that after many hours of interviews, a boss can reject a candidate after a five minute conversation (where the boss does most of the talking).

Recruiting, hiring, and firing has to be up to the people impacted by the action. Bosses add no value to it and only slow down the process.

Not Candidates

Almost from the start, we took the attitude at Nearsoft that candidates are already part of the team from the minute they voice an interest in the company. Even when we end up not hiring them, we need to treat each candidate as one of us. They want to be part of Nearsoft and they co-invest their time in our recruiting process so that makes them one of us.

We are transparent with candidates and they get detailed feedback at every stage of the process. I always felt that it was beyond arrogant to leave you in the dark and not to tell you exactly why you were not being hired even after many hours of interviews.

"Detailed" feedback means that candidates are told exactly what we feel they lack and ways to improve. We recommend books and websites that address the particular area and even have a mentoring/tutoring practice called Office Hours.

We want them to succeed in the long term and this is the kind of support that can help them going forward, at Nearsoft or elsewhere.

Growing the Community

Oftentimes, we may decide not to hire a candidate but one or more interviewers felt that she came really close. Maybe she came through as very curious and eager to learn or maybe she was most excited when she talked about solving hard problems. In these cases we usually offer to do Office Hours with the candidate. What this means is that a Nearsoftian volunteers to put in a couple of hours a week working with and mentoring her, assigning her exercises to do, books to read, solving problems together (*e.g.*, Pairing), etc.

Though the Office Hours program, we've "recovered" quite a number of these seemingly "failed" candidates. Also, the

Nearsoftians involved learn a ton in the process and get the satisfaction of mentoring somebody and watching her learn, grow, and eventually become a colleague. It's a real kick in the pants.

Even when they don't end up joining Nearsoft, people walk away with a much better feeling about the process and about themselves. More than once, they've recommended Nearsoft to their more experienced friends and relatives.

There are other cases where we hire more experienced people who are missing skills that we feel we can easily learn. In these cases, they get a full salary to go into what we call the Talent Incubator program. They get to work with a Nearsoftian who mentors them along the way. Remarkably, people tend to spend less time in the Incubator than what we expect.

All of these efforts help to grow the software development community which ultimately has helped Nearsoft grow. This mindset is not unique to Nearsoft. For example, Beetroot, a co-managed company in Ukraine, takes a similarly broad approach to growing the software community.[189]

Let Candidates Decide

Towards decentralization, we include candidates in some of the go/no go decisions we make along the way. For example, at the end of the English interview we have the go/no go discussion among interviewers *while the candidate listens.* For the most part, candidates remain quiet throughout, but other times the candidate joins the discussion. Their participation always weighs on the decision, and in a few cases, it has changed our minds and we've done a more extensive interview or talked at another time when the candidate is less nervous.

In a RADICAL company, you could, for example, experiment with involving candidates in the final hire/not hire decision. I've heard lots of objections to doing so, but we'll never know until we really try it. I have a strong suspicion that these concerns arise mostly from fear of the unknown.

Auditions

To take friction out of the recruiting process, some software companies use a process more akin to auditions than to interviews.

Software companies with products based on Open Source programs hire from the pool of people who contribute to the project. In this case, long term collaborations replace traditional interviews in these particular cases.

Menlo Innovations has a very unusual recruiting practice that they call Extreme Interviewing. They bring in a group of candidates at the same time and have them work in pairs, as is the norm at Menlo. From those, they invite a few to, "a full-day's audition, for pay, working on real client projects alongside two other Menlonians. The best of the bunch will then return for one more round of three-week paid trials."[190]

Automatic, the makers of WordPress, has candidates "… work for the company for three to eight weeks on a contract basis, doing real tasks alongside the people they would actually be working with if they had the job."[191]

Auditions, however, are not feasible for everyone. Not everybody can skip a few weeks from their current job to participate in a tryout. Having said that, it may be something that you'd want to experiment with.

Identity and Gatekeeping

The hire/no hire decision is made at what Nearsoftians call a Thumbs meeting, where everybody who's had contact with the candidate participates.

Using a 1-4 scale, every interviewer grades the candidate on two dimensions: technical expertise and cultural alignment. Most of the time, all the numbers come out close, but every so often, there appears a 1 in a sea of 4s or vice versa. That is where interesting discussions happen.

When the discrepancy is along the technology axis, there are fairly straightforward ways to deal with it. However, when the disagreement is over cultural alignment, things get more difficult.

Most times the outlier ends up changing his mark during the discussion and lines up with the others, although I've also seen the majority drift towards the outlier's view. Most times the difference is the result of confusion or faulty memory and others will bring out examples of why they gave the candidate a higher grade. Other times, it may come from misinterpretations or misunderstandings. Whatever the case, during the conversation people arrive at a common ground.

However, every so often, nobody moves one way or the other in which case the default decision is not to hire.

Is this a case of a minority imposing its will on the majority? Or as one author put it, "doesn't this take away the autonomy of the majority?" But this is not, I think, so much about autonomy as it is about team identity and team integrity. Preserving the existing team is more important than to risk its integrity by adding somebody to it who we are not sure is aligned with it. The existing team has learned to work together and that is worth preserving. Or maybe the problem is that team is dysfunctional—in that case, we need to address that issue before making things worse by adding people to it. What is clear is that 1) for a team to preserve its identity, a certain amount of gatekeeping is required, and 2) it is not easy to do.

Disrupting Recruiting

Co-ownership would dramatically disrupt how companies attract and retain people.

Today, every business is to some extent a technology business and they are having a difficult time finding people who can build their software platforms. When they do find them, they spend (waste?) a lot of time interviewing them. Once they are ready to hire them, they have to offer a big, juicy compensation package to join. And then, shortly after, they lose these precious people to Google, Apple, or Facebook for a bigger, juicier "package," including their brand appeal (*i.e.*, it looks great on a resumé).

Co-ownership changes that.

First of all, the brand pull will be significantly weakened. Regardless of their pedigree, the Googles and Facebooks of this world will not find it so easy to entice co-owners to leave *their* company.

On the other hand, FIAT businesses will be looked at with suspicion. "Oh, so I'd be just a worker bee?"

From our experience at Nearsoft, co-management alone is a significant attraction. As we started to be known as a co-managed company, people "picked up the phone" more readily and they even started to contact us!

Nearsoft's turnover has always been low and co-management has been a big factor in that. With co-ownership it could have been even lower, but we'll never know.

More about ESOPs

Louis O Kelso was a remarkable man. He recognized that poverty was a systemic problem and spreading ownership more broadly was the key to fixing it. He did everything in his power to give workers the ability to become owners, and to do so directly, not through the State. His idea was to have workers become owners of the companies they worked for, not by bloody revolution but by using the tools of Capitalism. Kelso showed up as a brilliant strategist in the same battlefield where Marx showed up as a poor tactician.

Henry George had a similar realization at the time that the main source of wealth was land ownership: "Land, labor, and capital are the three factors of production."[192] By the time that Kelso came along, businesses, not land, were the primary producers of wealth and capital. And businesses were not finite like land was, they were created out of capital and labor. Or as Kelso put it, "There are only two factors of production—capital and labor"[193]

Kelso experimented with ways of decentralizing ownership since 1956 and created a successful legal practice around it. He came up with what eventually would become the Employee Stock Ownership Plan (ESOP).[194]

In 1974,[195] with the enthusiastic support of Senator Russell Long, then Chairman of the Senate Finance Committee, the ESOP language got included in the ERISA Act.[196] A tool of capitalism, tax breaks, were used to make ownership decentralization attractive to workers *and* to FIAT owners.

The legislation lets FIAT owners sell all or part of their businesses to a trust, the ESOP, that is administered on behalf of its workers. ESOPs are tax exempt, and for FIAT owners this can be a biggie: "… in the right scenario, an ESOP can help your business avoid paying any kind of income tax at all."[197] This can be good for the workers, too, because "… the amount of money that's saved in taxes is enough to buy the business from the owner."[198] In other words, workers can buy the company using the company's earnings.

Once the owner is paid off, all earnings go into workers' ESOP accounts. This makes workers the financial beneficiaries of the wealth the company generates. Companies *could* be a training ground for workers to fully become owners, but, unfortunately, that's not at all part of the legislature.[199]

You would think that workers would be the primary buyers of ESOPs, but that's not the case. They are typically sold to FIAT owners, primarily as a tax avoidance technique. They can sell a minority stake of the business to the ESOP and can then reinvest the proceeds, tax free, in other companies.[200]

Government Regulation

Even the best intentioned government "solutions" are almost always expensive, and in more ways than one. As good as ESOPs can be, they come with their share of regulatory requirements and setting one up is expensive and time consuming. Running an ESOP is expensive, too, not only in terms of dollars, but also because of the legislative requirements. Most people who set up ESOPs for a living don't recommend it for companies with less than 20 people[201] or $500,000 in revenue. This means that new companies and small businesses can't take advantage of it.

Here's my simplistic understanding of how ESOP are administered,

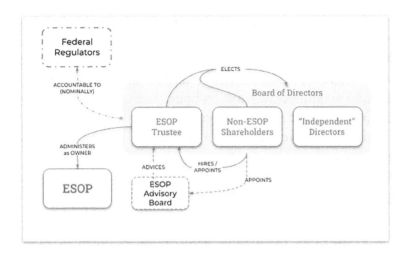

It involves lots of plan documents, ongoing reports, and lots of "fiduciaries" looking over each other's shoulders. It takes expert lawyers reviewing every action and specialized accountants to make sure everything is 100% CYA. This, some people would tell you, is what it takes to make sure the law is not abused because nobody will follow the rules unless compelled to do so.

The law allows for the FIAT owner to pretty much stay in control of the business. Or as one law firm puts it, "It's not a situation where everything changes. It does not transform employees into the Board of Directors. It does not disrupt the strategic planning or the various management hierarchies."[202] Translation: don't worry, you can do this and get the tax benefits, but the riff-raff won't be taking over any time soon. Even in the case where the ESOP owns 100% of the shares, the workers don't necessarily learn to be owners.

The share owner is the ESOP Trust, which is administered by a Trustee. This Trustee is a fiduciary hired by the Board whose job it is to look out "for the interest of" the workers. A benevolent parent who makes it all good for the little people.

There are a few cases of companies that have done it right, like New Belgium Brewery. Before they were acquired their ESOP owned 100% of the New Belgium shares. In parallel, New Belgium practiced Open Book Management, shared the company's numbers with everybody, and trained everybody on how to decipher the numbers. They involved everybody in financial decisions and annual planning. The return on this approach was that people were engaged, more productive, more inventive, and more resourceful. They were also happier and healthier. They were alive and their well-being spilled over into their adjacent communities.

In late 2019 the New Belgian Brewery workers, who by then were 100% the owners of the company stock through their ESOP, voted to approve the sale of the company to Kirin, the Japanese beer conglomerate. Evidently, these co-owners did what they felt was best for them and their business, just like any other owner would.

A Windfall

These days, ESOPs are most often pitched to FIAT owners as a Business Succession tool. "ESOPs have become the preferred tool of business succession and perpetuation for many S corporation owners."[203]

A retirement windfall, if you will. This would be great if it left the company in the hands of workers who were ready to run it. Unfortunately, most often this leaves the business in the hands of its bosses and leaves the body of workers unprepared to look after what supposedly is their property.

I found it somewhat surprising how big a carrot these tax exemptions can be. For example, a FIAT owner can sell shares to the ESOP and then reinvest this money tax free in Qualified Replacement Securities (QRS). These are nominally qualified US businesses. However, financial instruments like

Floating Rate Notes[204] have cropped up to get around this restriction and use this tax free money to diversify and invest in any business, including non-US businesses.

Rather than a tool to broaden capital ownership, they have become a tax avoidance haven for corporate bosses. Workers, the rightful owners, never learn to be full owners. To workers, it is pitched as a retirement fund, "keep doing your work and keep your eye on your growing pile of cash."

This would be well and good if this were only a transitional phase. Eventually workers would learn to be owners and that would spill over to benefit society. But that's not how it has worked out.

The FIAT owner or the top corporate bosses continue to run the business as their fiefdom and the wage earners never benefit from learning to be owners. They never engage at that level. The ESOP Trustee is supposed to look out for the interest of the workers. But since that's defined as their financial interest, so long as the workers' accounts grow in value, little else matters.

Kelso himself may have had higher hopes, but the Government did the only thing it could and created legislation that is all about money and taxes and nothing else. "Any organization that designs a system… will produce a design whose structure is a copy of the organization's communication structure."[205]

A key feature of RADICAL ownership is to have people *learn* to be owners. To benefit financially, yes, but also to learn to wield the tools and gain the benefits of becoming a full owner. *All benefits*, not just money.

Not Quite Co-ownership

We looked into a lot of things that sounded even remotely like co-ownership. Some of them have been combined in a few cases to create something very close, but by themselves none of them is quite it.

First, we must identify the FIAT system we have created and live in. This opens the door for alternatives, one of which is the RADICAL paradigm that we are espousing. It is not enough to make the FIAT paradigm more bearable.

Open Book Management: Not It

Open Book Management is a term coined by John Case in 1993. Open Book Management "is a catchall for a variety of approaches devised by companies looking for a more humane and more profitable way to operate."[206]

Jack Stack and a team of fellow managers at SRC Holdings branded their Open Book Management approach and spun it off as The Great Game of Business,

Publish and teach the rules	People need information and learn how to read it to make business decisions.
Create alignment tools	People need to align with their group. That's the job of the Impact, Purpose, and Mission of the organization. They are the only "boss" that counts.
Provide a stake in the outcome	The people behind the Great Game of Business clearly understand the value of equity and how it's different from a "bonus." Unfortunately, they present it only as a nice-to-have option: "One way to provide a stake in the outcome is through bonus incentives. Another is what is called equity sharing..."[207]

More than anything else, Open Book Management is about financial benefits and only a symbolic form of ownership. And, as Dr Corey Rosen has said, "symbolic ownership doesn't get you very far."[208]

Great Game of Business does understand the distinction between financial benefits and equity ownership,

> "The jury is in... companies that had awarded equity to employees saw sales grow 2.4% faster per year. Likewise, annual productivity growth increased 2.3% faster... an average increase in their return on assets of 5.5%, an increase in their net profit margin of 10.3%, and an increase in their return on equity of 5.6%... the average estimated productivity difference between companies that share equity and those that don't was 6.2%."[209]

The Great Game of Business goes a long way towards educating people on decentralization and transparency. They teach people to think and behave like owners, but they leave actual ownership as nice-to-have.

Its "Stake in the Outcome"[210] practice adds to the confusion. It is fairly well known by now that bonuses, commissions, and "incentive plans" in general are not conducive to teamwork and are counterproductive to actual performance.[211] They corrupt what usually starts as an intrinsic motivation ("that felt great?") and turns it into an extrinsic motivation ("I have to do this to get that bonus") manipulated by the boss.[212] A "stake in the outcome" is a commission by another name.

If we want to talk about ownership, then we must talk about an equity stake in the business. Equity is the only thing that reflects the value of the business *as a whole.*

For example, say you go and develop a new market for the business. My "stake in the outcome" may be 10% of the new business for a limited time, maybe a few months, or even a few years. But this new market increased the business's market value. However, since you don't have any equity in the business, you won't benefit from *that* growth, but the FIAT owners will. My "stake in the outcome" really is symbolic ownership that, "doesn't get you very far."[213]

CO-OPs: Not It

When we first looked at worker-owned cooperatives, I wasn't really enthused about them. I had visited Mondragon in Spain and a few worker-owned cooperatives around the Verona, Italy, region and I saw them as a partial solution at best. They were FIAT managed businesses with generous financial benefits for their workers. Nevertheless, Jose dragged me to the *2019 California Co-op Conference.*[214] We took Amtrak ride to Sacramento, California, and stayed at a nice Airbnb place (with a couple of growling, menacing dogs in the front yard).

The event started, as I expected, with an unmemorable lecture, full of dated, mid-last century imagery. It validated every one of my biases about "co-ops."

At lunch, I met people from various co-ops and my attitude started to change. I spoke with a couple of women from a cleaning co-op. Immigrants from Guatemala and El Salvador, they had come together as a co-operative and even made their own organic cleaning products. They were beaming at their accomplishments. It really put a smile on my face to see these people make so much out what little they had to start with.

Bottom line, I left the event with a different impression of cooperatives and a lot more hopeful that they could be a positive force and not just a relic of a bygone era. They, too, are about fixing our broken workplaces and many co-ops are searching for ways to remain relevant to that goal.

Many of the smaller co-ops we met at the conference were also co-managed but they did not describe it that way and that's because co-op people have a strong negative reaction to the word "management." The couple of times that I said, "oh, so you are co-managed," the reaction was immediate, "NO! We don't need managers, we organize our work ourselves." Later, I met people from Arizmendi and Rainbow Groceries and even though they are co-managed, they had a similar reaction: the word "management" was poison for them. In retrospect, it makes sense that "management" is bad and "organize" is good. Workers *organize* to get away from being exploited by *managers*. The last thing they want to hear is that they are managing. Yuck.

The thing that remained a concern for me is cooperatives' self-imposed blind spots around management and capital investment and their obsession with voting, "one member, one vote," as *the* governance tool. In spite of all the talk about democratic governance, co-ops are mum when it comes to FIAT hierarchy. Some have it, some don't. Some are co-managed when they are small and later end up with FIAT management because, "we are getting bigger now." In Northern Italy, the co-ops I spoke to were structured as FIAT hierarchies, even with traditional manager titles. In theory these bosses were elected. In practice, their top bosses have never been replaced. In one case, the same boss had been in control for 35 years. Mondragon, in Spain, is organized as a traditional FIAT hierarchy.

Unfortunately, without full participation in the running of the business, people might be financial beneficiaries but they are not owners and they don't *feel* like owners.

To further muddy the waters, not all co-op workers are co-op owners: Mondragon workers in the Basque region[215] are co-owners, but Mondragon workers in Mexico, the Philippines, Poland, etc, are not. They are simply employees, with no ownership rights.

LCAs: Not It

The relatively new Limited Cooperative Association (LCA)[216] model law allows capital investors into the cooperative mix. But there's a lot of controversy around them.

At one end of the spectrum, Ladislaus "Laddie" Lushin writes that the LCA model law can easily provide for capital investors, "to unilaterally organize, comprise, and control a closed pseudo-cooperative to the complete exclusion of all real patrons."[217] According to attorneys Dean and Geu, the model law would give, "investors substantial income and governance rights in the new business."[218] At the other end, according to attorney Linda Phillips,[219] the model law and its implementation in Colorado don't imbue investors with any particular rights, it all depends on the co-op's bylaws.

In any case, the LCA Model Act says nothing about co-management, except for the same vagaries about "democracy-as-voting" and in all other respects the language and paradigm comes straight from the legacy cooperative world.

ESOPs: Not It

Employee Stock Ownership Plans (ESOPs) are not well known, even though there are many of them out there.[220]

When I first learned about them, I thought I had found the foundation for co-ownership, but they are not it. They could be used as a legal umbrella for stock ownership, as it was implemented at New Belgium Brewing, but, in general, they are more often a legal sham.

When we first met Joeri Torfs and Pim Ampe in early 2019, they excitedly described their *Quality of Life Housing Project*.[221] It struck me that what they wanted to do for housing applied to any kind of ownership, including ownership of companies. I was intrigued and as I looked into it, I was surprised to find out that since the 70s there's been legislation in the US for this: the Employee Stock Ownership Plan (ESOP). The not-so-good news is that the workers don't actually own the stock. Evidently, the "workers" cannot be trusted with stock and the legal owner is the ESOP Trust. This Trust is administered by a Trustee and ultimately controlled by the Board. As explained in the NCEO website, "The trustee is usually also a named fiduciary and may be either a 'directed' or an 'independent' trustee... Most ESOPs use a directed trustee who acts at the direction of the company. Ultimately... the company's board of directors... has absolute authority over all retirement plan decisions"[222]

If the Trustee doesn't go along with the Board, the Board can fire the troublesome Trustee and get a new one. Such was the case with Ferrellgas, a liquid propane supplier. The business had an ESOP which owned 23% of the business stock. It was administered by GreatBanc as Trustee. Long story short, Ferrellgas got in trouble and ended up with $2.2B in debt. GreatBanc locked horns with the rest of the Board over how to dig out. The Board ended up replacing them. GreatBanc tried to block the replacement, but *the court sided with Ferrellgas* and denied the injunction request.[223] I don't claim to know who was right or who did best by the workers-owners. However, the fact that the Board could replace the Trustee does not pass the smell test for me. The whole idea of a Trustee, like a royal regent, running the ESOP on behalf of the little people just doesn't smell right.

What I got from this is that ESOPs function mostly "at the pleasure of" the Board and not so much "for the benefit of" the workers. But "what's good for the business" may or may not be "good for the workers." By law, and judicial practice, the Board has to focus almost exclusively on the financial performance of the business and their best financial decisions may not be good for the workers (*e.g.*, layoffs).

They can be part of the solution but, by themselves, ESOPs turn workers into financial beneficiaries, but not owners.[224] Dr Corey Rosen is the NCEO co-founder and has been an ESOP champion for many years. He has done a lot of research in this area.[225] At a Stanford University talk about worker engagement, he said that "symbolic ownership doesn't get you very far."[226]

It is interesting that, although he doesn't use the terms, Dr Rosen effectively says that co-management is more effective than FIAT management at creating wealth (*i.e.*, higher financial performance). Dr Rosen's own research shows that of all the factors, "... the most important was how participative the company was in the way it was managed. Did they have teams? Did they share financial information? Did they have their employees involved in day-to-day decisions? And those companies were growing about 8 to 11 percent per year faster whereas companies with a very top-down management were actually growing more slowly."[227]

Ostrom's Core Design Principles

I became aware of the work of political psychologist Elinor Ostrom a while back through one of the co-authors, Adrian Perez. He recommended a book by David Bollier, *Think Like a Commoner*, that included Ostrom's work studying as Commons, resources that don't belong to anybody and instead are stewarded by a community of users. She was the first woman to win a *Nobel Prize in Economics,* in 2009, "For her analysis of economic governance, especially the Commons."[228]

It was very interesting work but I thought back then that it only applied to the sea for fishing, open pastures where cattle feed, forests from which wood is extracted, reservoirs that provide water to communities, and the like. It didn't dawn on me that her framework was applicable to companies and not just Commons.

It has taken me this long to figure out RADICAL companies are the twenty first century Commons. She showed that successful Commons established rules for how they "are to be cared for and used in a way that is both economically and ecologically sustainable." The same applies to RADICAL companies and so her framework is equally applicable.

Ostrom framed her findings as a set of eight Core Design Principles that apply to all Commons, or as she called them, Common Pool Resources.[229] Like Commons, RADICAL companies are managed by the very people who embody them (co-management) and share the benefit of their bounties (co-ownership).

In the table below, the left column includes Ostrom's original description of each principle and the right column includes our interpretation of what each means for RADICAL companies.

	Ostrom's Core Design Principle	RADICAL Companies
#1	Boundaries of users & resources are clear	Clearly defined boundaries
	Individuals or households who have rights to withdraw resource units from the Common Pool Resources must be clearly defined, as must the boundaries of the Common Pool Resource itself.	Clear, explicit definition of 1) what determines who can be a member of a team or a company, 2) who has rights to extract wealth from the company, and 3) the company's constitutional framework that specifies what it is about (*i.e.,* Impact, Purpose, and Mission).
#2	Congruence between benefits & costs	Balanced contributions and benefits
	Appropriation rules restricting time, place, technology, and/or quantity of resource units are related to local conditions and to provision rules requiring labor, material, and/or money.	The balance of contributions, recognition, and other rewards must be trusted as fair and equitable.
#3	Users have procedures for making own rules	Inclusive Decision Making
	Most individuals affected by the operational rules can participate in modifying the operational rules.	Anybody affected by a decision must participate in making that decision.
#4	Regular monitoring of users and resource conditions	Monitoring

	Monitors, who actively audit Common Pool Resource conditions and appropriator behavior, are accountable to the appropriators or are the appropriators.	People are responsible for and accountable to each other. Regular check-ins are essential to the health of a team. Reviews and feedback are valuable gifts.
#5	**Graduated sanctions**	**Graduated sanctions**
	Appropriators who violate operational rules are likely to be assessed graduated sanctions (depending on the seriousness and context of the offense) by other appropriators, by officials accountable to these appropriators, or by both.	Misconduct must be dealt with gradually, with sanctions that range from the gentle to the harsh. Just as important is to deal with sanctions in a transparent and balanced way and to do so decisively and quickly.
#6	**Conflict resolution mechanisms**	**Conflict management**
	Appropriators and their officials have rapid access to low-cost local arenas to resolve conflicts among appropriators or between appropriators and officials.	In order to resolve conflicts effectively and inexpensively (both emotionally and financially), recognizing and voicing conflicts is an essential skill.
#7	**Minimal recognition of rights by Government**	**Right to co-manage**
	The rights of appropriators to devise their own institutions are not challenged by external governmental authorities. For Common Pool Resources that are parts of larger systems.	Co-management is an integral part of RADICAL companies, not the special characteristic of isolated teams.
#8	**Nested enterprises**	**Polycentric governance**

205

Appropriation, provision, monitoring, enforcement, conflict resolution, and governance activities are organized in multiple layers of nested enterprises.

RADICAL companies are decentralized and as such are governed policentrically. They also touch and are touched by many other adjunct communities including parent companies, subsidiaries, customers, candidates, industry peers, and the civil communities they are part of.

Why Are Boundaries so Important?

For Ostrom, the very first Core Design Principle is "Clearly defined boundaries." Who can fish in these waters, and who can't. Who can take water from this aquifer, and who can't. Who can bring their cattles to this pasture and who can't.

Dr David Sloan Wilson, a renowned evolutionist, worked with Lin Ostrom to show that "the Design Principles followed evolutionary theory."[230] Dr Wilson is also a co-founder of the PROSOCIAL Institute[231] along with Dr Paul Atkins and Dr Steven Hayes and they have expressed this Core Design Principle more generally as "Shared identity and purpose,"

> "This principle is fulfilled when everybody in the group feels as though they belong to the group and they share a belief in the value of its purpose. In practice, people often struggle to identify with a group when they don't believe in, or understand, its purpose."[232]

Clearly defined boundaries bind people into a common identity. "I am a fisherman in these waters."

FIAT Pyramids

For a FIAT managed company, "boundaries" really are the stone walls around the castle to keep would-be ransackers out.

Owners and profits are inside the pyramid's INNER level. This is damn near inviolate. For one, throwing an owner out is a big, big deal. It is doable, but it involves lots of litigation and such. Even kicking out a Director from the Board is a big deal. Golden Parachutes and other forms of monetary severance pay are often used to avoid litigation. All of this takes capital, time, and energy that otherwise could have been invested in the business.

The next level in the pyramid is for RESOURCES: human resources (*i.e.*, employees) and other assets. Moving employees in and out of this circle is costly and involves lots of friction. Bureaucracy thrives inside this level.

People are hired into this level as "at will" employees. Hiring is a stressful, high friction process where lots of existing employees participate, but the boss has the last word. Once the new employee is hired, the Human Resources (HR) Department sets them up for payroll, health insurance, issues a name tag, and, depending on rank, arranges for a desk, a small or shared office, or a corner office.

To fire a human resource out of this level, HR goes through a highly choreographed three-step dance and then the employee is out, sometimes with severance in exchange for signing a keep-your-mouth-shut agreement.

To bring an asset into this level, say, a laptop, the Purchasing Department issues a PO. It goes up and down the chain of command for approvals. If all goes well, Purchasing then buys a laptop from the lowest bidder.

The bottom is for TRANSIENTS: contractors, temporary staff, rented equipment, and the like. People and things move in and out of this level with a lot less friction because they are considered inconsequential to the business.

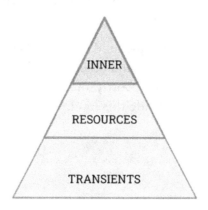

Note that customers are not part of the FIAT organization, ever. They are the raw material that the business harvests *wealth* from. All of which is under the sole control of the owners, inside the top of the pyramid.

As professor Sandy Pentland of MIT puts it in his book *Social Physics*, "the tragedy is that the negative externality from any individual's uncooperative action is experienced by the larger society, yet the benefit accrues entirely to the individual."[233] *Wealth* goes up into the top of the pyramid and *externalities* come out.

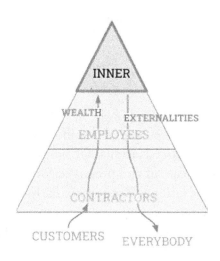

Most, if not all of this needless friction and its side-effects are a relic, a costly anchor that holds FIAT businesses back on productivity, flexibility, and innovation among others. In spite of it, FIAT businesses mindlessly go on paying this tax in exchange for the perception of control.

RADICAL Boundaries

Identity in a RADICAL company is more appropriately thought of as a function of alignment. It's not that the all-powerful "I" give "you," my subordinate, an identity. Rather all of us, align along a common Impact, Purpose, and Mission.

Impact is what the people who embody the company align with. I am aligned with National Geographic who wants the Earth being taken care of and preserved for generations. I am not aligned with National Geographic Partners whose goal is to make visually rich content that they can easily sell to more media outlets. The latter doesn't move me, the former does.

Different companies may have different Purposes, even if they want to make the same Impact. National Geographic and Patagonia were both born of love for wild beautiful places and they want to see those places preserved for generations, not exploited and destroyed. They are aligned on Impact, but Purposes are a bit different. National Geographic wants to bring these places to you, whereas Patagonia wants you to go to and experience these places.

A Mission is time-boxed, it has a beginning and an end. Once you've completed one, you'll need a new one and a company will have multiple Missions over time. At Nearsoft we defined one Mission for 2012 and another for 2017.

National Geographic's current Mission may well be to add drones to their image toolset, for example. Patagonia may also incorporate drones into their offering, but for people to record themselves while going through a unique experience. Same Impact, slightly different Purposes, different Missions.

Alignment

A clearly expressed Impact, Purpose, and Mission makes it easier to collaborate with other companies that are compatibly aligned. As David Logan explains in *Tribal Leadership*, these companies "while not the same, resonate with one another, so the organizations could work together... in the service of a noble cause that is bigger than what any company could pursue alone."[234]

In a piece for SheThePeople.TV, Ritu Yadva profiles "eco-friendly entrepreneurs,"[235] five young women intent on helping preserve our environment through the work their companies do.[236]

- Through tourism. Prerna Prasad, founder of Ecoplore,"urges people to explore nature in an eco-friendly manner and promote healthy living." Antara Chatterjee, founder of Little Local, promotes "volunteering while vacationing."

- By eliminating waste. Sahar Mansoor, founder of Bare Necessities, and Neerja Palisetty, founder of Sutrakaar Creations, are focused on zero-waste products and processes. Shagun Singh, founder of Geeli Mitti Farms, "is teaching the world to build cool, durable homes with mud and bamboo."

These five companies already are strongly aligned around a common Impact, to preserve the environment through their work, and could well work together as a Pod. As Nora Bateson, award-winning filmmaker, writer, and educator, has written, "let us think of boundaries ... as interfaces of learning."[237]

What about the Founders?

After all this stuff about co-ownership, what about the founders? Should they get special financial treatment?

After all, Roberto and I built Nearsoft from scratch. We bet on opportunities. We hustled to find clients. We kept one eye on revenue and the other on expenses. We managed to make the appropriate investments. We knew the market we wanted to serve and figured out how to approach it. Our strategy paid off, the company grew, and we had a successful exit. We did good as founders.

And that's the thing: the *role* of founder is a special one, but the *quality* of people who end up in that role is not. Our particular entrepreneur must have sharpened sensitivities, courage, and skills, but these were shaped by her circumstances and the communities around her. Her family, her neighbors, the schools she went to, and her social peer groups, all these elements and more formed our entrepreneur with the sensitivity to see the opportunity, the courage to pursue it in spite of the system we live in, and the skills to make it happen. However, she cannot pull the project off by herself and others must be ready to join in and make it happen. Because for the new idea to take root there must exist a whole lot of other folks at different stages of developing similar sensitivities, courage, and skills to join in a community with our entrepreneur and help make it happen.

The reason there are not as many founders around is because the FIAT system itself discourages people from showing up as founders. We've learned to scare each other out of taking risks. "What if it doesn't work, how are you going to live? Why not just get a real job and buy a nice car like your friends?" Don't be the nail that sticks out, it gets hammered down.

This is not done by bad people determined to keep us down, it comes from well-meaning people who want the best for us, starting with your immediate family. They, and we, are convinced that it is best to keep our gaze lowered and just do our jobs. Anything else is dangerous.

The FIAT system we live in throws up obstacle after obstacle, infantilizes us, encourages pathological codependency, etc. No wonder "founders" are few and far apart. Those special people are "winners" and the rest are "losers." The heads of the losers are put on spikes to make the rest of us tremble and think twice before following their steps.

Success and failure are highly determined by pedigree, luck, market conditions, and generally things that are not in our control. Maybe you win and become part of the FIAT establishment or maybe your head ends up on display along the road. However, it ends up, it has little to do with how *special* a particular individual is and has more to do with the circumstances that shape us.

We Took Risks

Yes, we, the founders, took risks, but not as many or as major as we'd like to think. And these risks also impacted everybody in the company, though as often as not it didn't occur to us to tell them. Unwittingly, we acted as "… the mere agent and trustee for his poorer brethren, bringing to their service his superior wisdom, experience, and ability to administer, doing for them better than they would or could do for themselves."[238]

On Roberto's side, there was a risk that Nearsoft wouldn't work and he would have ended up trailing his cohort. On the other hand, he graduated from a brand-name school and could at any point rejoin the rat race based on the friendships he had made there. Even more so, given who he is and what he is capable of, he would have likely ended up living the good life in the upper middle class anyway.

Most people would not dare take these risks, but Roberto did. He put on the line what little he had in a "crazy" adventure.

On my side, the risk was failing and not being able to rejoin the rat race. I was already over 50 when I started Nearsoft, so if it didn't work out, I was "doomed" to a life of highly paid gig work (*i.e.*, consulting).

Trying and failing was not a big issue for me. The area where I live, Silicon Valley, embraces failures. People here understand that the experience of trying and failing makes people 1) more capable, and 2) more respectful of those who have made it.

Our early clients, too, took risks. If we had gone belly up, it would be a major disruption for them (and we came perilously close in 2009) not to mention the loss of face that goes with choosing a business that goes under. "Why didn't you go with the service I told you about?"

The other Nearsoftians took risks, too, and shame was a big factor. "Why couldn't you just follow the rules? Shame on you." If things didn't work out, they could find a job, but their resume would carry the "shame" of having worked for a business that failed. "Why didn't you go to work for a serious business instead?"

Roberto and I have also done a lot of experiments that involved capital risks. We did this without consulting our co-workers or giving them any kind of a voice in the matter. Mind you, we didn't intend to do this in secret, and we didn't think of the general risk at the time. Nevertheless, they all took that risk along with us whether they liked it or not.

It's impossible to tell now, but I suspect that many of those decisions would have been different if we had included other Nearsoftians. As a larger decision team, we probably could have accomplished better results once everybody understood the risk we wanted to take.

We Saw the Opportunities

Yes, we did.

Roberto saw that software development was a business opportunity. He also saw that companies in the US paid more for the service, so he moved enthusiastically to find opportunities in the US. I wanted to build a company that I would have been happy to outsource to: geographically close by, time zone aligned, with high cultural affinity, and a dedicated team of people our clients would know by name and could talk to directly all the time. We felt that we could differentiate ourselves by offering a flat rate instead of the typical, complicated "rate card."

Other Nearsoftians saw opportunities, too. As they worked with clients, Nearsoftians pointed out things that Nearsoft could offer. In fact, most of our growth has come from existing clients who wanted more of what they were getting from their Nearsoftians.

We Led

People trusted and followed Roberto. He gave voice to their dreams. They believed that Nearsoft was the place "where the magic begins." We got clients to trust us, to believe that "closer is better," and to risk going with us.

But what made clients grow with us was not my magical charm or Roberto's resourcefulness. What made them stick with us was the people they worked with day in and day out. It was their competence, honesty, and attitude. They were all around good people and our clients wanted more of them.

We opened doors, but Nearsoftians made clients glad and confident that they had chosen to go with us. They turned every relationship into a long-term opportunity for Nearsoft. Our clients followed us because of our combined efforts.

We Hustled to Find Clients

Indeed. And for me, that was a real challenge.

I still hate rejection. It is one of the earliest strong negative feelings that I remember. Back in third grade we had a class election and although I did get elected, I did not end up as a top officer. At one point the class President asked the officers to come up to the teacher's desk and I got up. Before I could completely wiggle out of my desk, he said, "No, not you! Only *the officers*." As I write this, I still feel a small tug in my stomach.

I knew I had to get over the fear of rejection. Luckily, Jose Contreras, the first Nearsoftian, pointed us to the Sandler Sales Methodology class. It was life changing for me. It taught me to *search out rejection.* "Getting to no" was the skill I needed.

But getting new clients was only part of it. Retaining clients is even more important. All Nearsoftians have been integral to growing our client teams and therefore our revenue. Most importantly, they have made true believers of our clients. Our business has grown mostly on the basis of referrals and it all starts with how Nearsoftians show up with clients.

We Kept the Balls in the Air

A business is a perpetual balancing act. Revenue, expenses, investment, wealth extraction, well-being. A constant juggling that we did well enough.

This is one area where Nearsoftians didn't get much of a chance to participate. We will never know what opportunities we missed, how many risks we could have avoided, and, as they say, how much money we left on the proverbial table.

Greed or Recognition?

There may still be a case for giving the founders and a handful of early members a bigger piece of the financial benefits. We are not advocating this, but it may be something to be considered, at least for the time being.

- One way for founders to extract a bit more wealth is to get a bigger share of the annual Earned Dividends. A couple of co-managed companies I know use some form of this practice.
- Another way is to set up a Founder Banner that would allow people to recognize the Founders' original work

- You could also try to have a special "Founder RADs" factor at a higher multiple, for a given length of time. "… for the next 24 months Founder RADs will factor at 2x all other RADs." This could possibly be done as a transitional stage, from a FIAT economy to a RADICAL dominant one. People's habits and fears are ingrained and it might take something like this to accommodate them, so long as everybody knows what's going on and the practice may not harm others. If I get my extra portion out of your hide, then yes, you'd suffer and that would not be right. However, up to a point, if you get more than me, I'm not harmed if we both end up with more wealth than we would have otherwise.

We only mention these options for completeness, but we don't recommend any.

Another alternative is for founders to capitalize their efforts. "For what we've done, we deserve five million dollars." It would be treated like any other capital infusion that is "repaid" according to some terms.

VC: Founder-Making Machines

Different systems produce different results. The Venture Capital system produces more founders than the financing system that preceded it.

Once upon a time, investment money was called Risk Capital, until a few crazies changed its name to Venture Capital. As I moved from Chicago to San Jose, I went from "too high a risk" to my local bank to "not afraid of risk" in a venture. The change in labels reflected the different mindset of bankers versus venture capitalists and that alone removed a huge obstacle to new business creation.

The Venture Capital business sprung up on Sand Hill Road, Route 128, and a few other places.[239] At first, they were the target of ridicule, but then they won and became the establishment. It eliminated a lot of the obstacles that came along with the system of banks and wealthy "good ole' boys" clubs that preceded it, created a lot more founders, and became extremely financially successful.

I created my first business in Chicago, in 1980. At the time, I found one book, just one, that talked about starting a new business. It was all about getting patents, being circumspect, and showing that you are in charge. Steady as you go and don't do anything that might spook the bankers.

In spite of my ignorance, or maybe because of it, I went to my local bank to learn about what it took to get a loan. The woman who dealt with me at the bank was nice and all, but "do you have some form of collateral, a business or a house that you can pledge?" I think she knew the answer, but she had to ask.

The bank loan never happened, but I got started anyway. As a business it wasn't great, but it was paying the bills and my partner and I and our spouses loved what we were doing.

Almost two years later, one of our clients happened to come to Chicago. At dinner he told us how he had just gotten what sounded to us like a huge amount of money, or as he called it, Venture Capital. So, I asked him the same thing the nice woman at the bank had asked me, "Did you have to mortgage your house?" He looked at us like we were from a different planet. "No, it was a VC investment, why would they want my house?" Then he went on to tell us about his previous failed businesses and how the Venture Capital people found that valuable. It took the rest of our very long dinner for us to get a glimpse of what life on his planet was like. Less than two years later we moved to this new planet and landed in

San Jose, California. As I walked away from the plane, I shed my layers of clothing and have never looked back.

The most important difference in this new planet was that "doing" was a good thing. It was better if you succeeded, but they would not hoist your head on a spike if you didn't. "Great, now you know what not to do." Not having to worry (as much) about not spooking the money people was liberating. It sparked the imagination and opened new doors.

Silicon Valley was a huge lab with lots of experimentation going on. Mistakes and other obstacles were things that happened on other planets, not this one. Things that didn't work out were things to get past or go around, not obstacles that would stop you.

On top of that, these people wanted to spread the wealth. Back then in Chicago, a business's share of stock had an exalted quality to it and only a few executives got it. I remember our lawyer schooling us on the value of business stock in hushed tones. As far as I know, it was the Venture Capitalists of Silicon Valley who insisted that a stock pool for employees had to be part of the deal.

Altogether, the Silicon Valley system was more efficient at producing more founders than the system back in Chicago. Period. No special people required, just less obstacles than the old system. As Paul Buchheit, early Google engineer of "Don't be evil" fame, has said, "When we set everyone free, we enable the outliers everywhere. The result will be an unprecedented boom in human creativity and ingenuity."[240] The Venture Capital system has definitely done that.

Unfortunately, this system, too, has gotten encrusted with its own obstacles: its reliance on the FIAT hierarchy, its addiction to power and the perception of control, its narrow obsession with capital as the exclusive measure of success, and the implicit belief that money is the ultimate motivator.

The Ventura Capital system succeeded, got comfortable, and it stopped evolving.

We see RADICAL Investments as the next step in the evolution of capital investments. It should yield in total the same as today's VC system and it could potentially yield a lot more. In any case, it has less risk and a huge increase in the number of people who benefit from it and would be supportive of it.

3
RELEVANT NOTES

THESE APPENDICES ARE a few and most relevant of the many notes we took in putting together this book. Even though they never made it into the body of the book, we feel that they are significant and useful enough to append them to the book.

John Boyd

John Boyd was a military strategist and fighter pilot. He achieved many things, but he is best known for his "capacity for independent action" concept and the OODA Loop.

Retention

In his essay *Destruction and Creation*, Boyd points out that "... members may... remain independent, form a group of their own, or join another collective body in order *to improve their capacity for independent action.*"[241]

This phenomenon shows up most clearly in retention rates. To paraphrase Boyd, disengaged people are more likely to exit and go elsewhere where they can behave more like adults and control their destiny. Members of a RADICAL company are capable of expressing their voice, take meaningful actions, and do it as part of a group they are aligned with. They can make decisions and take action that is *independent* from a boss figure. This makes RADICAL companies more effective than FIAT businesses at retention.

WorldBlu, an organization which supports freedom centered companies, reports that retention rates at their companies far exceed the average in their sector. Our own experience at Nearsoft, supports the claim that having people engaged leads to higher retention rates than FIAT businesses.

Resilience

Co-managed companies are more resilient because they are more effective than FIAT businesses at navigating OODA Loop: Observe, Orient, Decide, and Act (OODA).

If two fighter pilots are going at each other, the one that goes through these stages more effectively, wins.

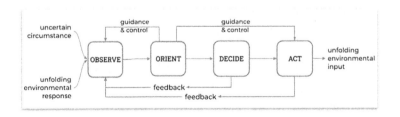

FIAT businesses give more salience to the *observations* of high ranked people, *decisions* are made by a few, and *actions*

must wait for approval. In a RADICAL company, *observations* can be made by anyone, *decisions* are made locally as needed, and *actions* don't have to wait for a higher up's permission.

Boyd's framework helps us understand why RADICAL companies have low turnover (high agency), are more resilient (many observing), and get better results (appropriate actions), including higher profits.

Sun April Fools Pranks 1985-1994

The April Fools pranks[242] were "the most notorious manifestation of Sun's freewheeling culture."[243] They are a good parallel to Sun Microsystem's arc as a business.

For 10 years people came together and self-organized with the goal of putting on one or more great April Fools pranks. Some years they were amazing, getting lots of press; others, not so much and they thankfully went quietly. If there was a purpose to them it was to 1) put together a fun event for all, and 2) to have fun while creating them. They went on this way until 1995. After that year, things changed, as author Karen Southwick points out, "... the tradition persists, although now the team that's going to do the joke is selected from employees who want to participate, and their target is also designated. Even the April Fools gags have become subject to a process."[244]

In other words, the April Fools events which started as a grassroot, self-organized effort became centrally controlled, with only "selected" employees "allowed" to participate. The events were forbidden in 1996 and when they were later brought back, the April Fools tradition was a shadow of its former self, much like Sun Microsystems itself.

The rows in grey include the year of the event, its theme, and its target.

1985	Office in Pond	Eric Schmidt

Eric's office is moved to the platform over the pond between Building 5 and Building 1.

1986	Car in Office	Eric Schmidt

A fully functional VW Bug "appears" in Eric's office in Building 5. He signs the title for it.

For all I know, he still owns it.

1987	Car in Pond	Bill Joy

Bill's car appears in the middle of the pond behind Building 6, resting peacefully on the surface of the water. Bill is given a dinghy to go rescue his car.

1988	Golf course in Office	Scott McNealy, Bernie Lacroute

Their offices in Building 6 were combined into a raised golf course, including a sand trap and a water fountain with a peeing angel.

Wayne Rosing teeing in the foreground. On the right, from left to right, Bill Shannon, Rob Gingell, and ?

1988	Office in Elevator, Birds in Office	Bernard Peuto
		Bernard Peuto's office in Building 5 was moved out to the elevator and his office was turned into an aviary. It even included a pair of peacocks, one of which dropped a doodoo on the workstation's keyboard just as a newspaper photographer was snapping a picture.
		Bernard really liked birds.

1989	Debugging Building 12	Eric Schmidt, OpenWindows team
		Building 12 was wrapped in plastic and "fumigated."
		A huge "NO BUGS" sign hanging from a crane pointed to the building and could be seen from Highway 101.

1990	All the Wood Behind One Arrow	Scott McNealy

A huge arrow through McNealy's office in PAL 1. It went out through one of the front windows. Scott and his visitors had to scoot under the giant arrow to enter his office.

And all because Scott spent the previous 12 months admonishing everybody to put "all the wood behind one arrow" (*i.e.*, don't use any CPU other than SPARK).

1991	Office in Pond	Wayne Rosing

Wayne's office in Steinhart Aquarium.

Wayne, in his scuba gear, sits in his underwater office while a shark swims right above him.

Thanks for the fish.

1992	SunPuck	Scott McNealy, Curt Wozniak

Sun execs were "fooled" into playing hockey with hockey luminaries like Bobby Hall. Sharks players attended and signed autographs (but at the last minute could not participate for legal reasons).

As the game starts Bobby Hall hooks McNealy who manages not to fall.

1993	Around the World	Bill Raduchel

Raduchel is made to look like he committed fraud. McNealy outs him at the annual VP/Directors Meeting.

It was actually painful to watch. But watch we did.

1994	Pond in Car in Office	Andy Bechtolsheim

A water tank full of catfish, in Andy's Porsche 911, inside his office.

The car was a bit longer than the office and we had to move a wall to make his office a few inches longer.

And that was the end of the office/water/car series. And it turned out, it was the end of an era.

Nearsoft Timeline

Our thanks to Iris Hernández[245] for helping me put this together.

Year	Peeps	Description
pre-2007		• Roberto founded what would become C Cube Technologies in Mexico. Later, Julio Gonzalez, Rodrigo Yañez, Diana Arvayo, and others join the team. • Matt founded Nearsoft as a California C Corp. Jose Contreras joins the team soon after. • Nearsoft and C Cube Technologies start to work together.
2007	8	• Nearsoft, US, merges with C Cube, Mexico.
2008	16	• Moved from "la casita" to an office in Hermosillo. • Ranked #6 by Great Place to Work™ (GPTW) in Tech in Mexico. This was the first time we signed up with GPTW.
2009	9	• The financial crisis hit us and it almost pulled us under. We laid off people. • Nearsoft is inducted in WorldBlu's list as a Certified Freedom-Centered Company. This was the first time we participated in their survey. • Read Maverick. • We watched Tony Hsieh give a Keynote at TIEcon 2009. • Started to formalize co-management at Nearsoft.

2010	~40	• The year starts as if the 2009 crisis had never happened. Sales picks up on the same upward ramp as of the end of 2008. • Everybody in the company participated directly in defining our Values. Roberto and I didn't participate for fear of biasing the results. • Leadership Teams debut. • Decision Matrix, inspired by Namasté's. • Transparency, full open books.
2011	~60	• The Nearsoft Academy is launched. A training plus mentorship model based on self-learning and a balance between personal, team, and technical skills.
2012	~85	• First 5-year Mission defined by the whole company. • First Team Building Day happened.
2013	~100	• Opened a new office in Mexico City. • Party to celebrate the 100th Nearsoftian.
2014	~125	• Moved into a new, custom office in Hermosillo built by the Rodriguez Foundation. The Foundation uses our rent to help pay for school for people of low means. Our price per square foot is lower, too. • First biannual Team Building Week. • People Development team launched.
2015	~150	• Opened a new office in the city of Chihuahua.
2016	~250	• Established a small team in San Luis Potosí and another in Merida. • Had our Spring Team Building Week in Cancun! • Celebrated the 200th Nearsoftian in July 2016.

2017	~300	• Launched offices for the teams in San Luis Potosí and Mérida.
		• More office space in Hermosillo.
		• Got acquired by Indecomm, Inc. Almost 200 people got to cash their stock! More than 20 became (MXN) millionaires.
		• New 5-year Mission defined at the Spring Team Building Day.
2018	~350	• Ranked #2 by GPTW in the technology sector.
		• Work starts on a new, bigger office in Chihuahua.
		• PEAK Teams launched.
2019	~370	• PEAK Teams spreading. They begin to include clients.
2020	~410	• COVID-19 happens.
		• Team Building Week in Cancún is cancelled due to COVID.
		• Work from Home for everybody starting the second week of March.
		• From the various acquisitions, Encora is launched as a global business.

4
WORTH MENTIONING

The Morning Star Company

The Morning Star Company is one of the poster children of co-management, and for good reason. Beyond co-management, the company has even taken some steps towards co-ownership, like having people set their own salaries in collaboration with their peers.

The other significant thing about this company is that their whole co-management system is based on, count them, two principles,

- No use of force
- Honor your commitments

This is very powerful, easy to remember, and simple enough to pass on to others easily.

1. No use of force

As we understand it, "No use of force" embodies Transparency and Decentralization. Keeping information secret, "on a need to know basis," is a form of violence.

Without decentralization, "force" is always present in one form or another. If you have the ability to fire me, then this is not a decentralized organization. "No use of force" requires a firm commitment to decentralization, which the Morning Star folks are committed to.

2. Honor your commitments

Honoring commitments is a key practice of decentralized companies, a basic skill for co-managers and co-owners. There are no bosses to chase after you, it's in your hands to honor your commitments. As an adult, we expect you to communicate if any obstacle is getting in your way, maybe we can help you remove them or go around it.

In addition, The Morning Start supports the following practices,

- No titles
- Colleagues, not employees
- No unilateral authority to fire [no violence]
- No command authority [no violence]
- Accountability process [honor your commitments]
- Freedom
- Coaching and mentoring culture

In a Corporate Rebels interview,[246] Doug Kirkpatrick, author, consultant, and member of The Morning Start founding team also listed out these practices,

- A collective of mission statements [Explicit alignment]

- The Colleague Letter of Understanding (CLOU) [Explicit alignment]
- Clear process to resolve conflicts (Core Design Principle #6).

Reinventing Organizations

Frederic Laloux is the author of Reinventing Organizations[247] The book has been received with lots of enthusiasm and has even engendered a movement of sorts.

Laloux wrote about 12 co-managed companies and categorized them according to this color scheme,

Description	Metaphor	Breakthroughs	Examples
RED			
Constant exercise of power by chief to keep foot soldiers in line. Highly reactive, short-term focus. Thrives in chaotic environments.	Wolf pack	• Division of labor • Command authority	• Organized crime • Street gangs • Tribal militias
AMBER			

Highly formal roles within a hierarchical pyramid. Top-down command-and-control. Future is a repetition of the past.	Army	• Formal roles (stable and scalable hierarchies) • Stable, replicable processes (long-term perspectives)	• Catholic Church • Military • Most government organizations (public school systems, police departments)
ORANGE			
Goal is to beat the competition; achieve profit and growth. Management by objectives (command-and-control over what, freedom over how).)	Machine	• Innovation • Accountability • Meritocracy	• Multinational companies Investment banks Charter schools
GREEN			
Focus on culture and empowerment to boost employee motivation. Stakeholders as primary purpose.	Family	• Empowerment • Egalitarian management • Stakeholder model	• Business known for idealistic practices (Ben & Jerry's, Southwest Airlines, Starbucks, Zappos)

TEAL			
Self-management replaces hierarchical pyramids. Organizations are seen as living entities, oriented toward realizing their potential.	Living organism	• Self-management • Wholeness • Evolutionary purpose	• A few pioneering organizations

The colors refer to an organization's "level of consciousness" which depends completely on the owner. As Laloux explains, "...the level of consciousness of an organization cannot exceed the level of consciousness of its leader." In other words, the FIAT owner shapes how the organization is run, how people behave, and even how they relate to one another. Co-ownership removes this limitation and lets the level of consciousness of a company emerge from the people who embody it, not just the owner/boss.

The book showed a lot of people that they were not alone in their wishing for a more just world. They could point to these companies as proof that their dreams and hopes were not fantasy. One of our early readers said that after reading Laloux's book "... my view of my own workplace changed."

Name	Sector	Location	Status	People
AES †	Energy	Global	For profit	40,000
BSO/Origin †	IT Consulting	Global	For profit	10,000
Buurtzorg	Healthcare	Netherlands	Non-profit	7,000

ESBZs	School, publicly funded	Germany	Non-profit	1,500
FAVI †	Metal Manufacturing	France	For profit	500
Heiligenfeld	Mental Health Hospital	Germany	For profit	600
HolacracyOne	Org Operating Model	US	For profit	
Morning Star	Food Processing	US	For profit	2,400
Patagonia	Apparel	US	For profit	1,350
RHD	Human Services	US	Non-profit	4,000
Sounds True	Media	US	For profit	90
Sun Hydraulics	Hydraulic Components	Global	For profit	900

† These were self-managed at the time but have since reverted to FIAT management.

Most of these companies are FIAT owned. As it happened with AES, BSO/Origin, and FAVI, once the benevolent owner/boss exits the stage they will more than likely revert to FIAT control.

As Laloux explains, his color scheme is derived from Ken Wilber's Integral Theory.[248] And, to my surprise, this relates it to Holacracy.

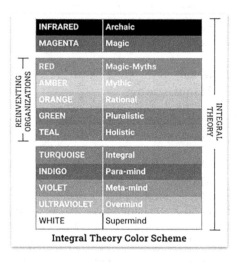

INFRARED	Archaic
MAGENTA	Magic
RED	Magic-Myths
AMBER	Mythic
ORANGE	Rational
GREEN	Pluralistic
TEAL	Holistic
TURQUOISE	Integral
INDIGO	Para-mind
VIOLET	Meta-mind
ULTRAVIOLET	Overmind
WHITE	Supermind

REINVENTING ORGANIZATIONS

INTEGRAL THEORY

Integral Theory Color Scheme

Holacracy

Holacracy is an alternative to traditional FIAT management. The three-piece-suit child of hippie Sociocracy always comes up whenever the topic of self-management gets discussed. But Holacracy is not a self-managed governance practice. Holacracy is strictly hierarchical and pretty bureaucratic.

Its Constitution exemplifies how bureaucratic the system is. The Holacracy Constitution can be many pages long (*e.g.*, 47 pages in one case) and it reads somewhat between a contract and a computer program. From the companies I've visited in the US and abroad using this system, I've noticed that people spend a lot of time picking and arguing over its many details. For one, keeping track of everybody's "roles" and when they apply can be a full time job.

Out of the box, Holacracy is a hierarchy of Circles where a given Circle has power over Circles below it. According to Steve Denning, consultant and author of *The Leader's Guide to Radical Management*,[249] "Holacracy is explicitly and strongly hierarchical."[250] That's the same impression I got after reading its Constitution and related documents. I had a chance to personally ask Tom Thomison,[251] a HolacracyOne co-founder, and he agreed that Holacracy replaced a hierarchy of bosses with a hierarchy of Circles. Brian Robertson, co-founder, of HolacracyOne and the public face of Holacracy, has said as much, "I would not describe Holacracy as a 'democratic' system, nor one organized around consensual democratic values. And it definitely doesn't seek to gain the personal consent of the workers for the organization's decisions."[252]

The good thing about it is that it leads people to take their first step away from the strict FIAT paradigm. Most of the companies I've talked to have moved beyond Holacracy and they either revert to the FIAT way of doing things or, more often, they move on towards their own flavor of co-management.

As an interesting tidbit, the name "Holacracy" is related to philosopher Ken Wilber's *Integral Theory*, although they are not as directly connected as some people think. In his book *The Ghost in the Machine* (1967) Arthur Koestler coined the terms *holon* and *holarchy*[253] and both Wilber and Robertson were inspired by it. "Wilber employs Arthur Koestler's notion of holons…"[254] and according to Robertson, "holarchy" is the root of "holacracy,"

Wobbly Developer @wobdev · Jan 2, 2014
Author @h1brian named #holacracy after the new age/mystical writing of Ken Wilber. holacracy.org/resources/inte… kenwilber.com/cultural/naked…

♡ 2

Brian Robertson
@h1brian

Replying to @wobdev

@wobdev Not true; the root of "Holacracy" is "holarchy", a term coined by Arthur Koestler.

en.wikipedia.org/wiki/Holarchy

4:39 PM · Jan 2, 2014 · Twitter Web Client

255

ABOUT US...

Matt M Perez

I'VE SPENT MY 40+ year professional career in tech. My work life has been bookended by Sun Microsystems at one end and Nearsoft at the other. They have shaped my beliefs about business and Capitalism, for very different reasons. The experiences I've had along the way, good and bad, underpin the RADICAL concept.

I started my first business in 1980. My main motivations were to 1) promote the technology I loved (Unix), 2) not have a boss, and 3) pay the bills. In that order. We hoped to make a living by making and selling our own software and from consulting.

Few businesses had even heard of Unix back then, but those that had needed all the help they could get. We found most of our clients on the tech-friendly West Coast. A few years later my family and I relocated from Chicago to San Jose, California, where I went to work for one of my clients. Fast forward to 1986 when I joined Sun Microsystems, one of the hottest businesses in Silicon Valley at the time. The business had a very dynamic engineering team, lots of opportunities to innovate, and lots of good and really smart people. It grew like there was no tomorrow and was generally a fun place. Sun's April Fool's pranks became legendary and were a very public expression of that fun.

At Sun I had the "opportunity" to live and see hyper-growth up close. Lots of bosses, each less effective than the previous one. For a while we knew our customers well—they were engineers, just like us. But then the business took a turn toward corporate sales and we were no longer clear as to who our customers were or even what business we were in. Corporate, nine-to-five types joined the business and we ended up less aligned over time.

Worst of all, trust was melting away. There was a shrinking top, a growing bottom, and many layers in between. Meaningless metrics. Unintelligible rules. Arbitrary salary distribution, "You have to remove the bottom 10% of your team annually."[256] HR became an executive shield. "Don't worry, I'll talk to him, but first sign here to acknowledge that there was no harassment." The "good" employees were the ones doing as they were told. The chance to innovate and do crazy things came to an end.

With time, I became worse as a boss and as a person. I was no longer the protector of people and had become the defender of my domain instead. I spent more time and effort looking out for number one and ended up not liking myself very much, although I didn't know it then.

I was in a meeting with a couple of peer bosses discussing a layoff and I wondered out loud about how the people who were not laid off were going to take it. One of my peers turned to me and said, "Why do you care?" And I thought, "Yeah, why should I care? I should learn from this guy!"

I quit soon after.

I continued on my acting-like-a-boss kick after I left Sun. It all looked pretty successful: VP titles, big salaries, lots of stock, lots of speaking opportunities, advisor to VCs, etc. But, all along, I could not shake the feeling that I was on a pretty sterile treadmill that only produced wealth while crushing everything else under its weight.

Over time I got off the treadmill and by the time Roberto and I started Nearsoft, about 10 years later, I was a very different person.

Adrian Perez

I have always been interested in what I would call the Third Way. It has seemed to me that often when dealing with a dichotomy, both sides are getting it wrong. You have two sides that are pushing and pulling over some territory and they get stuck in detente. This usually serves both sides, because it validates their survival. So whether it is traditional school or Montessori, Communism versus Capitalism, or any other such conflict, I look for the third way. In the case of schools, I found Sudbury Schools and Summersill. And for the case of how humans should organize their businesses, I have helped conceive the ideas in this book that we call Radical. The idea is to end the game that no longer serves us, so we can arrive at an idea that is new enough to create a whole new game. I enjoy shaking off the impediments of the older system and getting to an increase in human happiness, resilience, and power.

Having worked in software businesses in Silicon Valley, some in the ascendent and some collapsing, I have experienced the very informal and yet still very hierarchical, unimaginative, and stifling environments of corporate America.

We can do better.

It will take all of us, operating at our best to pull ourselves out of the nosedive that global civilization finds itself in. And I intend to help make the social tools we will need to free ourselves to operate at our maximum capacity for independent action.

Jose Leal

I started several businesses while I was in my late teens and rode the Internet wave, reaching that entrepreneurial dream – the successful exit. My business partner Ron and I joined the business, a top Canadian online media business, after our startup was acquired.

I never thought of myself as a boss but found myself in that situation. I had what many people would consider a dream job – Vice President and General Manager. The business was in the middle of another significant round of growth, hiring executives and hundreds of staff. The corporate budget was nearing dot-com era levels. There was another IPO push, the second in the ten years since we had joined the business. I recall saying, "I smell greed in the air." During the first IPO attempt, I was left to clean up mistakes made as things came to a crashing halt and everyone was thrown off the sinking ship. This time, I watched as those same mistakes were repeated and swore I wasn't going to do it again.

Just as Matt describes his experience at Sun, I hated not only the situation I was in but I hated myself. I had become everything I disliked about corporate types – a political, selfish, heartless hatchetman – at least outwardly. Inwardly, it was killing me and exacting a tremendous toll on my body and personal life. In short, I was a complete mess. Just in time, I was able to negotiate my exit. Within the year, the executives and hundreds of staff were gone.

I quickly jumped back in and co-founded my fourth startup in the online marketing space. Initially, I was thrilled to be away from the corporate life and diving back into a new project. But as I look back on that time, I realize my heart was never in it. Every time things started to look promising, I lost interest. It dragged on for years. Eventually, both the startup and my marriage were coming to an end, and I was numb to it all.

While spending many months back in my birthplace of Portugal, helping to take care of my mother after her stroke, I dove deep into figuring out what had happened. I felt like I was finally starting to come out of the fog I had been in for years. The impact of those ten years had been worse than I had imagined and I couldn't understand how it had happened. How I had become so lost?

I've spent the last several years researching and studying what makes us human and what prompts us to certain actions and choices. A couple of years ago, I had the good fortune to get connected with Matt and we had a meeting of the minds. Together, we are fleshing out the RADICAL concept and are developing better approaches to organizing companies. Our vision is a future where traditional FIAT hierarchy no longer grinds people into submission but rather the new realities of co-management and co-ownership give people and organizations the opportunity to flourish.

Glossary

GLOSSARY

"If you want to create new behaviour, you often have to use new language."

—*Vicky Saunders, founder of ShEO*[257]

AS YOU PROBABLY noticed, we've used unusual terminology throughout this book. Co-management instead of self-management. Co-ownership to refer to our decentralized notions of ownership. And heavy use of the word FIAT to put a label on something that has mostly remained unnamed and invisible. Also, we unapologetically use the word "boss" instead of the more polite "manager" or the Orwellian "leader," to refer to people with power over others derived from a FIAT hierarchy.

Boss

When referring to people empowered by FIAT to command others, we call them boss instead of "managers" or "leaders."

We know many people who have the title of manager who don't behave as bosses. They are good people trying to be a positive force, but they are in an untenable position. This book is in many ways meant for them.

Real leaders embody an Impact, give voice to the team's Purpose, and support the team's Mission. That's why people enthusiastically follow them. We're not talking about them. We are talking about people whose primary function is to wield power.

Anthropologist, and author David Graeber calls them bullshit jobs, "Yeah I got a bullshit job, I'm in middle-management. I got promoted. I used to actually do the job, and they put me upstairs and they said supervise people, make them do the job. And I know perfectly well they don't need somebody to supervise them or to make them do it. But I have to come up with some excuse to exist anyway."[258]

Those who are assigned the power to command and control others are bosses and can never escape being bosses. We have lived through that and if you have the title, you are a boss.

The boss role has come to include some useful functions, but these functions can be done, usually better, by multiple people. For example, the boss is usually the person responsible for conflict resolution. But there are other ways of dealing with conflict that are decentralized, more consistent, and more sustainable over the long-term. A boss can tell you that you are moving in the direction that's most beneficial to him; but explicit, transparent alignment tools are more dependable and consistent.

Capitalism

"Capitalism is a limited and shorthand analytical device that only partly explains our unequal world alongside a range of others, including patriarchy, hierarchy and alienation."
—*Andre Pusey, Beyond capitalist enclosure, commodification, and alienation*[259]

Throughout this book, we use the term "capitalism" to refer to the system for collaborating with others to create bigger and more impactful results than we could accomplish on our own. An Open Source project is as much of a capitalist act as a company; in one the investment comes as sweat equity, in the other as capital. You don't have to agree with this "definition," that's just how we see it.

Conventional belief tells us that "capitalism has done enormous good" and has served "to eliminate needless suffering." But it also "has given us too unstable a society" and it "needlessly produces or perpetuates" suffering.[260] Capitalism has been *brutal*, particularly in the Americas.[261]

Capitalism is perceived in many ways. If you are well off, it's great, otherwise, it's not. But even that is too simplistic. Billionaires like Warren Buffet speak about the many things that have gone wrong with our kind of Capitalism. On the other hand, there are many, even among the very poor, who sing its praises because they expect to be "one of the big guys" one day.

At the risk of oversimplifying, we started by working together in small bands of extended families. At some point, we replaced voluntary affiliation with violence and forced others to labor for us by slavery and indenture. Later, we replaced physical violence with currency, and although that was generally for the better, currency is a more subtle form of violence.

Our present form of capitalism seems immutable, to the point that "It seems to be easier for us today to imagine the thoroughgoing deterioration of the earth and of nature than the breakdown of late capitalism; perhaps that is due to some weakness in our imaginations."[262] But it isn't.

Besides capital aggregation, Capitalism is based on our concept of property. And changing *that* is what co-ownership is all about.

Company

Throughout this book we use the word "company" to refer to people who come together to create something uniquely human. A "corporation" refers to a legal structure and a "business" to what a corporation makes, trades, or offers as a service. They are both associated with "capital." A "cooperative" or "collaborative" puts the emphasis on "labor." Instead, "company" puts the emphasis on people. The word comes from *com-* and *panis*, Latin for a group of people who break bread together. This is a powerful image of people who have come together around a purpose.

The people who embody the company are aligned along its explicit Impact, Purpose, and work together to complete their Mission. A company is about making promises to each other, to customers, and to everybody they touch. A RADICAL company is not only about the work people do and how they organize responsibilities (co-management), but also about sharing the wealth and the requisite risks (co-ownership) that result from their work.

As we use it, "company" includes for-profit and not-for-profit organizations. Big ones and small mom-and-pop shops. Product and service companies.

We use the words *company* and *workplace* interchangeably as appropriate.

Co-Management

We use co-management instead of self-management because a company does not manage itself. A company is managed *collaboratively* by the people who embody it. An individual can self-manage but a company is co-managed by its members.

There can be no such thing as a self-managed team within a FIAT organization. There may be teams that "are given permission" to manage themselves ("I don't care how you do it, fix the problem") but these are usually short-lived. These may go by different names, such as Emergency Task Force, Kamikaze team, or Tiger team. Otherwise, the whole idea of a self-managed team encased in a FIAT organization doesn't make any sense. Like a school of sardines surrounded by hungry dolphins, it won't last long.

Hierarchy doesn't go away (*i.e.* there's no such thing as a flat company), but it is not imposed from a monarchic top. Leadership and hierarchy emerge organically whenever people interact, given the local conditions, and needs.

Another reason we avoid the term *self*-management is that it can mean different things in different contexts. Search for it online and you'll find references to self-care, self-control, self-regulation, etc.—all to do with individuals, not organizations.

Co-management is decentralized management in every sense of the word.

Mary Parker Follet had used the term co-management in her book *The New State*,[263] published in 1918. In that instance, she was referring to the collaboration of owners and workers managing a company. Evidently, she assumed the separation would continue and hoped instead that working together in committees would allow each to see the other as people.

Co-Ownership

We use co-ownership instead of "democratic ownership" or the more traditional "cooperative." The former, "democratic ownership," is too amorphous and the latter, "cooperative," too rigid.

Co-ownership has been used in the past to mean government ownership (*e.g.*, nationalized industries in the UK and Europe after WWII, in Russia after 1917, and in China after Mao Tse-tung). Evidently these writers could not conceive of decentralized ownership in the hands of people, but we were not in their shoes and it would be arrogant to judge them.

Today, co-ownership is occasionally used as synonymous to a partnership or some other oligarchic agglomerations of ownership, "created under general incorporation statutes that allow such fictitious legal persons to engage in a wide variety of profit making."[264] At the other end, in the European Union, co-ownership refers to enabling citizens to "become (co-) owners[sic] of the utilities that supply them."[265]

In this book, the term co-ownership stands for a model of ownership that is decentralized, dynamic, and includes all company contributors. It is about sharing all the wealth that a company generates (*e.g.*, cash, assets, brand, equity, etc.). It is about sharing the responsibilities, risks, and decision making.

Cultural Fit

"Fit" usually is a euphemism for "people like me," or "people I like," or even "people I can control." It is not what we want.

In a healthy place, we don't all come in to work at the same time, we don't wear uniforms, and we are not soldiers doing the goose-step. We do bring our whole selves, including our weirdness, or as Nilofer Merchant calls it, our "onlyness," to work. A healthy workplace is not a mold that you have to *fit* into along with all the other cogs.

Alignment seems like the more accurate term. We have to be *aligned* in order to pull in the same direction.

Democracy

The term "democracy" has come to be interpreted in so many ways that it has become less than useful, to put it mildly.

For one, democracy is often conflated with voting, "one person, one vote." But democracy, "which has been made to bear such a burthen of incongruous notions,"[266] is about participating in *shaping* the questions, not simply choosing between A or B.

All in all, co-management seems like the more accurate term to describe that we are managing our work collaboratively.

Earned Dividends

We use Earned Dividends instead of Profit Sharing[267]

First, there's revenue. Then, what's left after paying for the cost of goods, expenses, and the like is net profit. From it, the business retains a chunk to capitalize the budget for the following year. What's left is the wealth generated by the company that can be distributed to the owners as dividends.

Normally, the execs and shareholders take the biggest chunk of these dividends; sometimes they leave some to be distributed as "profit-sharing." But this is no longer "profits," these are dividends. Also, it is not a bonus or any kind of gift from Mount Olympus, it is wealth that everybody in the company has *earned* through their contribution to the growth of the company.

I thought that we had come up with this label but then I remembered that I had already heard it from Garry Ridge, CEO, WD-40[268] It took me nearly 10 years to understand what he patiently explained to me back then at a WorldBlu event.

Employee

We also avoid certain words like pests because, in fact, they are mental pests, the kind you don't want bouncing around in your head. "Employee" is one of those words.

The word "employee" has its roots in *plicare*, meaning to bend or ply. You could say that "employee" is someone who bends to another's will[269]

People who work for a living as employees of FIAT businesses are indentured to the boss and as such they are not at all free during work hours. Even their "non-working hours" are for the most part devoted to eating and resting so they can go back to "bend to another's will" the next day.

Experimenting

We thrive in a culture of shared learning and personal growth, where it is safe to experiment. The result of an experiment, whatever it is, never is a *failure*. The problem with the FIAT mindset is that it doesn't allow for experimentation at all.

An experiment sounds like this, "Let's do X and we think we are going to get Y, otherwise we'll learn from it." That is unintelligible in a FIAT environment. Instead, every utterance is a firm commitment to be passed up the chain of command as an immutable promise. *Failing* to meet that "promise" leads to loss of face for your boss and, likely, punishment for you.

Family

"I treat my employees as I treat my family." That's paternalism, not co-management.

Ricardo Semler's father was a good person and he treated his employees well. Ricardo Semler, the son, did away with it and went all out into co-management and a good distance into co-ownership.

Employees are disposable resources, they are not at all family. "Family" doesn't get fired when it's convenient.

FIAT

FIAT is, admittedly, not the kind of word that rolls off the proverbial tongue. People often misread it as "FLAT" or mishear it as "FEAR."

Fiat comes from Latin "let it be done," from the word *fieri*, "be done or made." In English, it means a decree or arbitrary order, in other words, FIAT is about the power to issue decrees and give arbitrary orders. Kings did it by FIAT, and so do bosses today.

FIAT hierarchies[270] gum up the works wherever you find them, and you'll find them most everywhere. It is the normal thing, the way it's always been, the way the world works. It is the dominant paradigm and a wasteful tragedy.

FIAT Management

"Drowning people
Sometimes die
Fighting their rescuers."

— *Octavia Butler, Parable of the Sower*

A FIAT managed business is organized as a FIAT hierarchy where everybody is assigned a title and a measure of power by FIAT.

The FIAT hierarchy is expensive. It slows down productivity, it eliminates flexibility, and discourages innovation. It is a tax that, for some reason, FIAT businesses insist on paying in exchange for perceived control.

FIAT Ownership

We were very surprised that there isn't an umbrella term for the various forms of private ownership of businesses. We have sole ownerships, partnerships, and various forms of corporations. But I could not find a term for all of them as a class.

So, we call these FIAT *owned* businesses.

What's common to FIAT owned businesses is that, by the divine rights of capital, all the wealth produced by the business flows up to the owners. Money, brand, equity. Everybody else involved in making a business happen gets paid what they get paid until the boss decides otherwise.

As author Marjorie Kelly so well put it in her book *The Divine Right of Capital*: "This is the law of the land, much as the divine right of kings was once the law of the land.

In the dominant paradigm of business, it is not in the least controversial."[271]

Although they are led by enlightened people who are courageous enough to step outside the box, most co-managed companies today are FIAT owned. Nearsoft was.

Flat

Flat is not the antonym of FIAT, there is no such thing as a "flat" group of people. I have confused these two in the past. Whenever people gather together, hierarchies form organically and they come and go dynamically and fluidly. In a FIAT organization the hierarchy is *imposed* from "above."

This much was obvious to Jo Freeman an attorney, political scientist, and feminist. In her classic, *Tyranny of Structurelessness*, she writes, "Any group of people of whatever nature that comes together for any length of time for any purpose will inevitably structure itself in some fashion. ... The very fact that we are individuals, with different talents, predispositions, and backgrounds makes this inevitable."[272]

There even is a physics law to back that up. According to professor Dr Adrian Bejan, if there are two or more people involved, there's a flow, from high to low. "Hierarchy is unavoidable and impossible to efface."[273] For example, when two people talk there's a flow of information from person A who may know *more* about a topic to person B who knows *less*. The problem with FIAT hierarchies is that the flow is pre-imposed by rank: the boss tells the employee what's "right" and the employee has to defer to rank, regardless of who knows more about the topic.

Freedom

Unfortunately, the word "freedom" has been co-opted and as Victor Frankl points out, "… freedom is in danger of degenerating into mere arbitrariness."[274]

All in all, co-management seems like the more accurate term. Whether or not somebody else wants to call this freedom, what we are doing is having the ability to manage our work collaboratively.

Indenture

We hesitate to use the word *indentured*. It comes from Latin *indentare*, from *en-* (in, into) and *dent* (tooth). In other words, to be "indentured" means to be in somebody's grip.[275] That is pretty close to the position that most of us find ourselves in as wage earners.

It is "normal" for most of us today to indenture ourselves to a FIAT owner who will pay us "what the market bears." In the "gig economy," people indenture not only their time and labor but also things that they own (*e.g.*, cars, motorcycles, bicycles, their homes). FIAT businesses extract wealth from it all and keep most of it, much like a feudal landlord extracted rent from his land and the people in it.

Of course, today we are free to move to another business anytime, our bosses don't own us quite as rigidly as the Lords of yore. But it is not always easy to leave a job, and sometimes it is practically impossible (*e.g.*, during pregnancy).

You may be thinking that Uber and the other Unicorns would have never come to pass if we waited for the unwashed masses to make them happen. It required the smarts and bravado of the founders together with the investors' capital and courage. And, yes, in our FIAT world, this is the way it is. But the RADICAL paradigm is about reshaping the world so the alternative is more likely and the wealth generated by our combined efforts is distributed equitably.

Member

Members of a co-owned company include the people who embody the company. Besides the people who contribute their work, members include capital investors, customers, and anybody else who identifies with and is aligned with the company.

The distinction between member and co-owners is subtle: co-owners are the members who have been allocated RADs. Their contributions have been recognized by other co-owners and have been allocated RADs. All co-owners are members.

I borrowed the term "member" from Ernest Bader, founder of Scott Bader, who thought of a company as a community "of which his employees would be *members*."[276]

Open Book Management

Open Books Management[277] is a term coined by John Case in 1993.

It "is a catchall for a variety of approaches devised by companies looking for a more humane and more profitable way to operate."[278] In practice, it is about teaching people about the critical numbers, how to read them, and how they related to each other. In many cases, it also involves financial benefits related to meeting or exceeding certain key indicators. But it does not include building equity in the business that people help grow. It is merely symbolic ownership.

Educating people on how their work affects the value of the company is a big productivity win. But as NCEO founder

Dr Corey Rosen has said, "symbolic ownership doesn't get you very far."[279]

Pods

As they grow, RADICAL companies become polycentrically governed. Decision "centers" come and go fluidly, as the people involved and local conditions require. What holds them together as a company is their explicit alignment (*e.g.*, Impact, Purpose, and Missions).

They also align at different levels with the communities they are part of: customers, candidates, industry peers, etc. We call these things Pods.[280]

We first thought of it as a network, but "network" doesn't quite convey what they are. Network categories may apply but only briefly because Pods are fluid, dynamic.

Whether the term will stick or not is not the point. The important thing was to have a handle for this new kind of organization that we believe will form out of primordial RADICAL soup.

RADICAL

I had some resistance to the word at first. A couple of the people who read the manuscript were concerned that the term would turn people off.[281] After some discussion, we decided to stick to it and here is more or less why,

1. The word derives from *radix*, the Latin word for root. In the political realm it means "unconventional change from the roots."

2. The audience for this book is people who sense that something needs to change, at work, in politics, in our lives.

These people are looking for a radical change, not a different shade of lipstick for the pig. Ours is a different take on it, one that points to non-violent ways to effect change, the radical type.

3. The book by Ricardo Semler, Maverick, got Roberto, my partner, and me oriented to this way of thinking. As it happens, the book Maverick is called *RADICAL* in Spanish.

4. The current system, the FIAT system, needed a name to give it a shape and make it visible and therefore replaceable. RADICAL in this sense is the antonym of FIAT.

5. When used as an *adjective* it can be used in combination with familiar words like management, ownership, and governance.

We don't want to mince words or make up a completely value-free, acceptable-to-all term. As an example of the latter, consider *the chaordic governance system*. It is the name that Dee Hock gave to the VISA governance system which brought a new, creative twist to corporate organization and a pioneer in corporate land. Unfortunately, the *chaordic* label didn't connect with people. People who have talked with Mr Hock directly have told me that he didn't want to scare the bankers he needed to sign up to the VISA model. Whatever the reason, the term *chaordic* never made it out of obscurity.

We don't know if RADICAL-as-adjective is going to stick, and that's not important. But we won't get out the gate by holding back.

Self-Organizing

Elsewhere in this book we've explained that "self" implies that the organization is a thing on its own. But it is not, and it doesn't organize itself.

With all due respect to the people who hold it dearly, "self-organizing" is dated, often related to the "labor" and "cooperative" movements of the past century. Yes, they were valuable for their time, but they got stuck as separation movements: more power to labor, less for owners. But owners and laborers are people, not distinct species.

Finally, we want to get this message in front of people who happen to have the title of "manager." They can be a force in making this change. The authors have been managers at one point or another, so there's hope.

Self-Governance

Elsewhere in this book we've explained that "self" implies that the organization is a thing on its own. But it is not, and it doesn't govern itself.

Co-management obviously includes governance as well but we didn't want to risk people conflating it with "government." Elsewhere in this book we've talked about that, when it comes to social change, "government" is where good intentions go to die.

Slavery

We are loathe to use the word slavery except in its appropriate context. Nothing compares with its sheer brutality and "inexpressible cruelties."[282]

Yes, we are trapped in a FIAT system that limits our option, but, no, it is nothing like slavery.

ENDNOTES

1   Renamed Encora Nearshore by the time you read this. https://www.encora.com

2   For more references, see DOT-COM Bubble. https://radicals.world/nO7aTa

3   Ben Geier. What Did We Learn From the Dotcom Stock Bubble of 2000?. March 12, 2015 https://radicals.world/lFa66V (alt. https://diigo.com/0hodmv)

4   Marc Andreessen. Why Software is Eating the World. August 20, 2011. https://radicals.world/QlhBnv (alt, https://diigo.com/0i9uli).

5   For more references, see The Year 2000 Problem. https://radicals.world/uVFlnV

6   Based on Trancept Systems), founded by Nick England, Mary Whitton, and Tim Van Hook. Sun acquired Trancept as an acquihire, before that name came into vogue. https://radicals.world/o3i8Aw (alt, https://diigo.com/0imaks)

7   Sun Microsystems Inc 10-K Annual Report. https://radicals.world/9nBgPx (alt, https://diigo.com/0g43oz)

8   Today we would call this a time-boxed release. Obvious as it may sound now, the idea was fairly new back then. James Martin had already written about it in 1991 in his book, Rapid Application Development. https://radicals.world/Y7veoI

9   Robert Jackall. Moral Mazes. 1988. https://radicals.world/azz9Hv

10 Chuck Blakeman. Rehumanizing the Workplace. 2020. https://radicals.world/0QO0zs

11 See The Global Financial Crisis in 2009 for more references. https://radicals.world/RPNprB

12 See The Force for more references. https://radicals.world/awO0pg

13 For more references, see Maverick. https://radicals.world/M3x22N

14 Logan et al. Tribal Leadership. June 7, 2011. https://radicals.world/me9oOC

15 Chip Conley. PEAK. 2007. https://radicals.world/JHgvVR

16 Matthew Kelly. The Dream Manager. 2007. https://radicals.world/rxaJVU

17 Dennis Bakke. The Advice Process. 2012. https://youtu.be/vUaDD9mnXVI?t=24

18 For more information, see Nothing About Us Without Us. https://en.wikipedia.org/wiki/Nothing_About_Us_Without_Us

19 David Marquette. Leadership Nudge™ – Above and Below the Waterline. The term seems to have originated with W L Gore and Associates. https://radicals.world/3UM9hu

20 Elinor Ostrom. Lee Kuan Yew School of Public Policy – Beyond Markets and States. 2010. https://youtu.be/E5ZPGeF2ics?t=625

21 Douglas McGregor. The Human Side of Enterprise. 1975. For a summary, see appendix Theory X, Theory Y. https://radicals.world/cNbgKp (alt, https://diigo.com/0fnzpe)

22 NetMBA Business Knowledge Center. Theory X and Theory Y. https://radicals.world/1w2VQb (alt, http://www.netmba.com/mgmt/ob/motivation/mcgregor/)

23 Douglas McGregor. The Human Side of Enterprise, p 2. 1975. https://radicals.world/cNbgKp (alt, https://diigo.com/0fnzpe)

24 State of the Global Workplace. Gallop Report, 2017. https://www.diigo.com/item/pdf/zk1n/1xpv

25 Paul Buchheit, engineer, entrepreneur, investor, ex-Sun Microsystem, creator of Gmail, and ex-Facebook. https://radicals.world/xoDqyt

26 Umair Haque, Betterness – Economics for Humans. https://a.co/3q3Hlrv

27 Catherine Clifford. Hedge fund billionaire Ray Dalio: "Capitalism basically is not working for the majority of people". CNBC's MakeIt, Jan 16, 2019. https://radicals.world/I2mCJ7 (alt, https://diigo.com/0i9udg)

28 This attitude has been called "business unionism" by James Dennis Hoff in 'No Power Greater': Solidarity and Struggle

at CUNY. It has also been called the "common good" view by Alan Gillies in Software Quality: Theory and Management. https://radicals.world/kUAh1U (alt, https://diigo.com/0h207e) https://radicals.world/U3flll (alt. https://radicals.world/n0cpxN)

29   Ryan Shomer, Lar Desouza. Least I Could Do [NSFW]. September 5, 2019. Permission to use granted. https://radicals.world/LbjiUi

30   Tyson Yunkaporta. Sand Talk. 2020. https://a.co/5zWVdrk

31   Mark Carney, governor of the Bank of England. By invitation: Mark Carney on how the economy must yield to human values. 2020. https://radicals.world/b75wQ7 (alt, https://diigo.com/0imae3)

32   Peter Leeson. The Invisible Hook: The Hidden Economics of Pirates. 2009. https://a.co/3H78JQV

33   For more references, see Post–World War II economic expansion. https://radicals.world/qXYLAy

34   Scott Bader Constitution. https://radicals.world/5BXSNh (alt, https://www.diigo.com/user/matt_perez/b/547882995)

35   The Gore Story. https://radicals.world/eJIK7k (alt, https://diigo.com/0i9udl)

36   Bernhard Schroeder. What Is the Magic Number of Employees in a Startup or Company, in One Location, Before Tribalism Begins to Break It Apart?. Feb 2020. https://radicals.world/Fslg4k (alt, https://diigo.com/0iejxh)

37   Gary Hamel. Building an Innovation Democracy, p 9. https://radicals.world/WckPSC (alt, https://www.diigo.com/item/pdf/zk1n/9cn3)

38   Gary Hamel. Innovation Democracy: W.L. Gore's Original Management Model. 2010. https://radicals.world/pZ3CId (alt, https://diigo.com/0iejxm)

39   James Huston. The American and British Debate Over Equality, 1776-1920 (Kindle). 2017. https://a.co/1Ptmem0

40   The Electoral College had no legitimate purpose once the 13 Amendment was adopted. https://radicals.world/xvVEHg

https://radicals.world/WrvSoC

41 Dr Joseph Blasi. A Founding Father Profit Sharing Fix for Inequality. April 14, 2017. https://radicals.world/bW7MUU (alt, https://diigo.com/0imafi)

42 Peter Drucker, Management: Tasks, Responsibilities, Practices. 1973. https://radicals.world/tGgi8I

43 Kim Jordan, in an interview by Lucas Li. New Belgium Brewing tour + interview with CEO Kim Jordan. Nov 14, 2011. https://radicals.world/tBw5tK (alt, https://diigo.com/0h1qo7)

44 See appendix ESOP. For more detail, see More about ESOPs.

45 The New Belgium ESOP was first established in 2000 when it owned 35% of the company. In 2005 it owned 42%, 47% in 2012, and in 2017 the ESOP became the sole owner of the company.

46 The Foundation for Enterprise Development. Directed by Passage Productions (52 minute). We the Owners: Employees Expanding the American Dream, a film by Infobase Learning / Films Media Group. https://radicals.world/SQPLB2

47 Ironically, in 1917 Russia had the smallest proletariat in all of Europe. Most of their population was eking a living off the land, not working in factories.

48 For more references, see Henry George. https://radicals.world/0dFYy9

49 For more references, see Progress and Poverty. For the original, see Progress and Poverty. https://radicals.world/qburBQ https://www.diigo.com/item/pdf/zk1n/qh70

50 For more references, see San Yat-sen. https://radicals.world/SZIPs1

51 Wikipedia Commons. Political performance art by Fay Lewis in Rockford (Illinois), 1914. https://radicals.world/GlK2oV

52 Henry George. Progress and Poverty. 1879. https://www.diigo.com/item/pdf/zk1n/qh70

53 Francis Peddle, PhD, Philosophies of Integration: Sun Yat-Sen and Henry George. https://radicals.world/ncBKEC

54 Pierre Lemieux. Land Taxes: The Return of Henry George. 2018. https://radicals.world/cZc5p6 (alt, https://www.econlib.org/land-taxes-the-return-of-henry-george/)

55 See Lizzie Magie for more references. https://radicals.world/Q12lGp

56 Lizzie J Magie. The Landlord's Game. Patented Jan 5, 1904. https://radicals.world/5ybTQl (alt, https://diigo.com/0i9uer)

57 John Bates Clark, The Philosophy of Wealth (Kindle). 1886. https://a.co/e0nZ821

58 Remarks of Honorable Charles Eckert of Pennsylvania in the House of Representatives. Eckert, Henry George – Sound Economics and the 'New Deal.'. Tuesday, July 2, 1931. https://radicals.world/o84Yrz (alt, https://www.diigo.com/item/pdf/zk1n/tybj)

59 Remarks of Honorable Charles Eckert of Pennsylvania in the House of Representatives. Eckert, Henry George – Sound Economics and the 'New Deal.'. Tuesday, July 2, 1931. https://radicals.world/NjQS37 (alt, https://www.diigo.com/item/pdf/zk1n/tybj)

60 Remarks of Honorable Charles Eckert of Pennsylvania in the House of Representatives. Eckert, Henry George – Sound Economics and the 'New Deal.'. Tuesday, July 2, 1931. https://radicals.world/NjQS37 (alt, https://www.diigo.com/item/pdf/zk1n/tybj)

61 Remarks of Honorable Charles Eckert of Pennsylvania in the House of Representatives. Eckert, Henry George – Sound Economics and the 'New Deal.'. Tuesday, July 2, 1931. http://scarc.library.oregonstate.edu/omeka/items/show/10806 (alt, https://www.diigo.com/item/pdf/zk1n/tybj)

62 Remarks of Honorable Charles Eckert of Pennsylvania in the House of Representatives. Eckert, Henry George – Sound Economics and the 'New Deal.'. Tuesday, July 2, 1931. http://scarc.library.oregonstate.edu/omeka/items/show/10806 (alt, https://www.diigo.com/item/pdf/zk1n/tybj)

63 See, Georgism for more references. https://radicals.world/XhT9wT (alt, https://diigo.com/0iig3b)

64 Annika Neklason. The 140-Year-Old Dream of 'Government Without Taxation.'. Atlantic, April 15, 2019. https://radicals. world/ceAbXD (alt, https://diigo.com/0jrtrn)

65 The Foundation for Enterprise Development. Directed by Passage Productions (52 minute). We the Owners: Employees Expanding the American Dream, a film by Infobase Learning / Films Media Group. https://youtu.be/6sszYBw8tYo?t=106

66 Seth Godin. What kind of org?. May 4, 2020. https:// radicals.world/WlO6ji (alt, https://seths.blog/2020/05/ what-kind-of-org/)

67 That's what has been written widely, but I have not personally verified it.

68 Gary Hamel and Michele Zanini. Yes, You Can Eliminate Bureaucracy. HBR 2018. https://radicals.world/WI3wdk

69 Valve: Handbook for New Employees. https://radicals.world/ JMfg2K (alt, https://diigo.com/0gta1p)

70 Joost Minnaar. The World's Most Pioneering Company of Our Times. Corporate Rebels, 2018. https://radicals.world/ IIEJpD (alt, https://diigo.com/0hfysm)

71 Chuck Blakeman is the author of Making Money Is Killing Your Business and Why Employees Are Always a Bad Idea. https://radicals.world/4Xx2G8 (alt, https://radicals.world/ LM14eE)

72 Jing Hu and Jacob Hirsh. Accepting Lower Salaries for Meaningful Work. Frontiers in Psychology, 29 September 2017. You can find lots of similar works online. https://radicals. world/27ufgg (alt, https://radicals.world/980PFP)

73 Alexandra Anderson. Twitter post. May 9, 2020. https://twitter. com/alexandersonmd/status/1259327416926908423

74 Nilofer Merchant. Should You Say No to that Big Job Offer?. Feb 4, 2020. https://radicals.world/pYrd9D (alt, https://radicals.world/GUBzQa)

75 Brené Brown. The power of vulnerability. TEDxHouston. 2010. https://radicals.world/uy3lKE

76 Nilofer Merchant. Should You Say No to that Big Job Offer?.

Feb 4, 2020. https://radicals.world/pYrd9D (alt, https://radicals.world/OTZ3Vm)

77   This is also a gesture popularized in The Hunger Games movies to express unity with people striving to survive. Since 2014 it has also become a symbol of pro-democracy in Thailand. Very apropos. https://en.wikipedia.org/wiki/The_Hunger_Games https://radicals.world/pG9bAM (alt, https://diigo.com/0iu409)

78   Dave Logan. How to Develop Your Noble Obsession. Aug 5, 2013. https://culturesync.net/how-to-develop-your-noble-obsession/ (alt, https://diigo.com/0ia7ug)

79   Luis Ortiz. Work Hard, Have Fun: a Day-in-the-Life at Nearsoft. https://nearsoft.com/videos/life-at-nearsoft/

80   Luke Hohman. Innovation Games: Prune the Product Tree. For how we played the game at Nearsoft, see Prune the Product Tree. https://www.innovationgames.com/prune-the-product-tree/

81   Luis Ortiz. Work Hard, Have Fun: a Day-in-the-Life at Nearsoft. 2016. https://nearsoft.com/videos/life-at-nearsoft/ (alt, https://diigo.com/0j6zps)

82   See appendix Recruiting for more references.

83   See Philip Rosedale for more references. https://en.wikipedia.org/wiki/Philip_Rosedale

84   Nicolas di Tada. Salary compensations without intermediation. Manas Blog, Dec 13, 2018. https://radicals.world/B4Jolk (alt, https://diigo.com/0ipx3j)

85   Our thanks to Nathan Saicheck for bringing up this question.

86   Jessica Sillman, quoting Phil Rosedale in Why Employees Should Decide Who Gets Bonuses. https://radicals.world/t1P8ht (alt, https://diigo.com/0h10y6)

87   James Owen. Drawing Out the Dragons: A Meditation on Art, Destiny, and the Power of Choice. 2014. https://radicals.world/KjVrI5

88   Jessica Sillman, quoting Phil Rosedale in Why Employees Should Decide Who Gets Bonuses. https://radicals.world/KjVrI5 (alt, https://www.diigo.com/user/matt_perez/b/574995418)

89 Sanford DeVoe, Sheena Iyengar. Medium of Exchange Matters: What's Fair for Goods Is Unfair for Money. 2010. https://radicals.world/KjVrI5 (alt, https://www.diigo.com/user/matt_perez/b/574995418)

90 Warm Data is a concept developed by Nora Bateson. For more information, see the Warm Data Labs site. https://radicals.world/W6M7zt)

91 Michael R A Chance. Social Fabrics of the Mind, Michael R A Chance, Ed. 2015. https://a.co/7pip7pR

92 Michael R A Chance. Social Fabrics of the Mind, Michael R A Chance, Ed. 2015. https://a.co/ivUwBf9

93 Michael R A Chance. Social Fabrics of the Mind, Michael R A Chance, Ed. 2015. https://a.co/2IwsOyt

94 Michael R A Chance. Social Fabrics of the Mind, Michael R A Chance, Ed. 2015. https://a.co/2PSFmPh

95 Chuck Blakeman. Rehumanizing the Workplace by Giving Everybody Their Brain Back. 2020. https://radicals.world/kegSnn

96 Jack Rimington. Twitter post. Feb 5, 2020. https://radicals.world/IgOfJa

97 Seth Godin. Born to run (things) alt., here). Jan 14, 2021. https://seths.blog/2021/01/born-to-run-things/ (alt, https://diigo.com/0jgole)

98 Jack Stack, The Great Game of Business. https://youtu.be/S0qw_GX8I5A?t=431

99 Jack Stack, The Great Game of Business. https://youtu.be/S0qw_GX8I5A?t=431

100 Ricardo Semler, Maverick. 1988. https://radicals.world/ANgLYQ

101 Jie Li, Bruce Boghosian, and Chengli Li. The Affine Wealth Model: An agent-based model of asset exchange that allows for negative-wealth agents and its empirical validation. 2018.

102 Bruce M Boghosian, Is Inequality Inevitable?. November 2019. https://radicals.world/xI17kA (alt, https://diigo.com/0fsqtw)

103 Bernard Lietaer, Jacqui Dunne. Rethinking Money: How New Currencies Turn Scarcity into Prosperity. 2013. https://a.co/954O96N

104 Bernard Lietaer, Jacqui Dunne. Rethinking Money: How New Currencies Turn Scarcity into Prosperity. 2013. https://a.co/954O96N

105 See Fagor for more references. https://en.wikipedia.org/wiki/Fagor

106 See Mondragón for more references. https://en.wikipedia.org/wiki/Mondragon_Corporation

107 Joost Minnaar. How to Rapidly Scale a Mission-Driven Company without Selling Out. October 2020. https://radicals.world/kzy8j7

108 BuurtzorgT website. https://radicals.world/hIDLRS

109 Steward-ownership. Purpose Foundation site. https://radicals.world/mXBU3C

110 Armin Steuernagel. Transforming Ownership to Create a Better Economy. TEDxZurich, 2018. https://youtu.be/Z2Uy_ODDiZo?t=19

111 ESOP (Employee Stock Ownership Plan) Facts. https://radicals.world/350pGH (alt, https://diigo.com/0ibkhg)

112 WorldBlu's Freedom at Work model. https://radicals.world/350pGH (alt, https://radicals.world/45G5wX)

113 ESOP (Employee Stock Ownership Plan) Facts. https://radicals.world/350pGH (alt, https://diigo.com/0ibkhi)

114 Bernard Paranque and Hugh Willmott. Cooperatives: Saviours or Gravediggers of Capitalism? The ambivalent case of the John Lewis Partnership. 2014. https://radicals.world/ElFHKk (alt, https://www.diigo.com/user/matt_perez/b/545671545)

115 Nikil Saval. Utopia, Abandoned. August 29, 2019. https://radicals.world/apwgQc (alt, https://diigo.com/0ipwxj)

116 Sociocratic Democracy. https://radicals.world/W3ny8W (alt, https://diigo.com/0ipwya)

117 Gerard Enderberg, as quoted in Beyond the Bottom Line:

Socially Innovative Business Owners. https://a.co/1gc5YIT

118 Edward Albert Filene. https://radicals.world/gJXwrb (alt, https://diigo.com/0jc3xr)

119 Jack Quarter. Beyond the Bottom Line: Socially Innovative Business Owners. 2000. https://a.co/f4qTN3u

120 Mary Parker Follett. The New State. 1918. https://a.co/h8Berdd

121 Elinor Ostrom – Facts. The Nobel Prize site. https://radicals. world/izty4z (alt, https://diigo.com/0ia7y5)

122 Dr Paul Atkins, course material. PROSOCIAL Facilitator Certification. 2019. https://radicals.world/uhEMi7

123 Franz de Waal. Two Monkeys Were Paid Unequally. Apr 4, 2013. https://radicals.world/dOgzRK

124 Most of the HR folks are genuinely good people who went into this role to help others. Indeed, they very often are the ones who lead implementation of good, high impact programs. In the end, though, their job is to shield the business and top execs from lawsuits.

125 James Barker. Tightening the Iron Cage: Concertive Control in Self-Managing Teams. Administrative Science Quarterly, Vol 38, No 3, Sep 1993. https://radicals.world/wFNe3c (alt, https://www.diigo.com/user/matt_perez/b/545734494)

126 Richard Bartlett. Bootstrapping a bossless organisation in 3 easy steps ;-). May 19, 2016. https://radicals.world/bAJsmz (alt, https://diigo.com/0ia7re)

127 J Kim Wright. Lawyers as Changemakers: The Global Integrative Law Movement. year. https://a.co/eLM7JKw

128 WeI highly recommend Nonviolent Communications by Marshall Rosenberg. https://en.wikipedia.org/wiki/ Nonviolent_Communication

129 Zulema Salinas. Twitter Post. Aug 19, 2020. https://radicals. world/0hdf5J

130 Robert Kegan. The Further Reaches of Adult Development – Robert Kegan. YouTube, https://radicals.world/7YX6h3

131 David Klein A Brief History of American K-12 Mathematics

Education in the 20th Century. 2003. Emphasis added. https://radicals.world/Ws9frS

132 The whole "mind-body problem" is coming under scrutiny and my sense is that it's time to retire it. See the works of Dr Georg Northoff and others. https://radicals.world/V8ZDF6

133 Emphasis added. Geert Hofstede. Dimensionalizing Culture, The Hofstede Model in Context. 2011. As Hofstede has said many times, this is a measure of culture at the national level and makes no claims below that, certainly not at the individual level. https://radicals.world/Q6XnLF (alt, https://www.diigo.com/item/pdf/zk1n/bjr2#)

134 Hofstede Insights. What about Mexico?. https://radicals.world/4GlJIs (alt, https://diigo.com/0hoplf)

135 Pablo Aretxabala. Las 10 estructuras básicas de la autogestión según nuestro NERbyK2K. Jul 24, 2020. https://radicals.world/28Izg8 (alt, https://diigo.com/0iezem)

136 Liqueed, Happyforce, 10Pines, Basetis, Manas, UruIT, Pressto Tegu, Grupo Cygnus, Vagas, Grupo Anga, Semillas del Caribe, Grupo Qualia, Zero Transportation https://radicals.world/ml9YQO https://radicals.world/JWLYDK https://radicals.world/yQixnw https://radicals.world/SVV6RG https://manas.tech/ https://uruit.com/ https://radicals.world/cJNcMK https://tegu.com/ https://www.cygnus.cl/ https://www.vagas.com.br/ http://www.grupoanga.com/ https://www.semillasdelcaribe.com.mx/ http://www.qualia.mx/ https://www.zarotransportation.com/

137 Joost Minnaar. VkusVill: How A Russian Giant Disrupts The Retail Industry. Corporate Rebels Blog Jan 2, 2021. https://corporate-rebels.com/vkusvill/

138 Lisa Gill. Episode 42, Ved Krishna on self-management in an Indian paper factory. Feb 3, 2020. https://radicals.world/vx0jjy

139 Ved Krishna. Nature Based Packaging. TEDxPSITKanpur, March 24, 2018. https://youtu.be/cxQc6Mz_c3U?t=41

140 Pradeep Chakravarthy. Management & Leadership: Lesson from Temples. July 9, 2019. https://www.youtube.com/

watch?v=ak6avSg0CEE

141 Suresh Pandit. https://www.linkedin.com/in/sureshpandit/

142 James Barker. Tightening the Iron Cage: Concertive Control in Self-Managing Teams, p 3. 1993. https://radicals.world/5eO2C9 (alt, https://www.diigo.com/user/matt_perez/b/545734494)

143 Richard Edwards. Contested Terrain: The Transformation of the Workplace in the Twentieth Century, p 22. 1979. Emphasis adde https://radicals.world/skz6a3 (alt, https://radicals.world/l8qAZS)

144 Gary Hamel and Michele Zanini. Humanocracy (Kindle). 2020. https://a.co/cSy5PSK

145 Jonathan Haidt. The Righteous Mind. March 13, 2012. http://a.co/3Z6EDHK

146 Tyson Yunkaporta. Sand Talks: How Indigenous Thinking Can Save the Word. May 2020. https://a.co/0bVttP2

147 Richard Sheridan. Joy, Inc: How We Built a Workplace People Love, p 3. 2013. https://a.co/dmpCgNX

148 John Holloway. Change the World Without Taking Power. 2013. https://a.co/ivS7wlx

149 Gallup Report. State of the Global Workplace. 2017. https://radicals.world/UjEXuV (alt, https://www.diigo.com/user/matt_perez/b/537244593)

150 Dr M Hayes, Dr F Chumney, Dr C Wright, M Buckingham. The Global Study of Engagement Technical Report. 2019. https://radicals.world/ib50vR (alt, https://www.diigo.com/item/pdf/zk1n/w6g1)

151 Doug Kirkpatrick, author of: Beyond Empowerment, 2017; From Hierarchy to High Performance, 2018; The No-Limits Enterprise, 2019; Essays from the Edge, 2020. https://radicals.world/YUSRh8 https://radicals.world/j76Iqu https://radicals.world/6jFr3D https://radicals.world/JyhC75

152 Doug Kirkpatrick. Interactive Periodic Table of the Future of Work. https://radicals.world/1B2TH7

153 Umair Haque. Betterness: Economics for Humans. 2011.

https://a.co/5gfGxjl

154 Lisa Gill interviews Gary Hamel on Busting Bureaucracy for Good in her podcast Leadermorphosis. https://radicals.world/gTNXVl (alt, https://radicals.world/XWnF7f)

155 Frederic Laloux' response in the comments to Bursting the Bubble: Teal Ain't Real. https://radicals.world/535gKO (alt, https://www.diigo.com/item/pdf/zk1n/c1iy)

156 SenseTribe mentions it in their Guide and the Great Game of Business movement talks about it, too. https://radicals.world/yfv9tp https://radicals.world/MVbHCq

157 Seth Godin. When can we talk about our systems? (alt. here). September 24, 2020. https://radicals.world/E46PwG (alt, https://diigo.com/0ijnru)

158 Nilofer Merchant. Should You Say No to that Big Job Offer? Feb 4, 2020. https://radicals.world/NAbUVW

159 Mike Moyer. Slicing Pie website. https://radicals.world/Vi9ZCF

160 Mike Moyer, Slicing Pie at Stanford University. https://youtu.be/pLGDba8aSWE?t=225

161 Mike Moyer. Slicing Pie at Stanford University. Mar 17, 2014. https://youtu.be/pLGDba8aSWE?t=3809

162 Mike Moyer. Slicing Pie at Stanford University. Mar 17, 2014. https://youtu.be/pLGDba8aSWE?t=3254

163 Slicing Pie, Version 2.3. Page 128 (70%).

164 Bram van der Lecq. No More Ass-Kissing: An Alternative Salary Model. Corporate Rebels blog, 2020. https://radicals.world/0EAqzu (alt, https://diigo.com/0ipx52)

165 Nicolas di Tada. Salary compensations without intermediation. Manas Blog, Dec 13, 2018. https://radicals.world/B4Jolk (alt, https://diigo.com/0hjq18)

166 Pim de Morree, Corporate Rebels. Self-Set Salaries: A Practical Guide. 2018. https://corporate-rebels.com/self-set-salaries/

167 Maciej Gałkiewicz. What I've learned as a CEO from a year of self-set salaries. May 8, 2018. https://radicals.world/SPbB0b (alt, https://diigo.com/0ipx5r)

168 Liqueed, Happyforce, 10Pines, Basetis, Manas. https://radicals. world/ml9YQO https://radicals.world/JWLYDK https://radicals.world/yQixnw https://radicals.world/SVV6RG https:// manas.tech/

169 See Board of Directors for more references. https://en.wikipedia.org/wiki/Board_of_directors

170 Tom Peters. Twitter post. Aug 2, 2017. https://twitter.com/ matt_perez/status/892850058428911618

171 Edmund Burke. Reflections on the Revolution in France [PDF]. https://radicals.world/5oY7Tu

172 Lisa Gill interviews Gary Hamel on Busting Bureaucracy for Good, 9:40. https://radicals.world/PeVZ7x (alt, https://www.youtube.com/watch?v=Q4X_JuTtwjg&t=494s)

173 Warren Buffet, Chairman. Letter to 2019 Berkshire's Shareholders. February 22, 2020. https://radicals.world/qTd80m (alt, https://www.diigo.com/item/pdf/zk1n/3y78)

174 Louis O Kelso, Mortimer Adler. The Capitalist Manifesto. 1958. https://radicals.world/W1HncK

175 Dr J Robert Beyster, Peter Economy. The SAIC Solution: Built by Employee Owners. May 28, 2014. https://a.co/dkEwTbK

176 Dr J Robert Beyster, Peter Economy. The SAIC Solution: Built by Employee Owners. May 28, 2014. http://a.co/8N2369p

177 Dr J Robert Beyster, Peter Economy. The SAIC Solution: Built by Employee Owners. May 28, 2014. https://a.co/glwHCcS

178 This idea comes directly from Joeri Torfs and Pim Ampe.

179 K2K Emocionando. https://radicals.world/KozIZu

180 The NER Group. NER stands for Nuevo Estilo de Relaciones or New Style of Relationships. This "new style" is very close to what we call co-management. https://radicals.world/tEaXbr

181 Pronounced kut-cha. See Carmen Larrakoetxea's NER Group crea Kutxa Ner, un modelo de financiación empresarial alternativo a los bancos. El Economista, March 3, 2015. https://radicals.world/EwGRNp (alt, https://diigo.com/0irvcd)

182 Max Weber. The Protestant Ethic and the Spirit of Capitalism

and Other Writings. 1905. Translated by Peter Baehr and Gordon Wells. https://a.co/4yig0e8

183 Thanks to J Kim Wright for the thought, so beautifully expressed. Private communications.

184 Bruce Peters, private communication.

185 Tim Ferris. Ricardo Semler—The Seven Day Weekend and How to Break the Rules (#299). March 19, 2017. https://radicals.world/XSSPVD (alt, https://diigo.com/0hobm1)

186 As quoted in Sand Talks by Tyson Yunkaporta. John Zerzan is an American anarchist, primitivist ecophilosopher, and author https://a.co/jcWXmC8

187 Douglas McGregor. The Human Side of Enterprise, p 1. 1975. https://radicals.world/McCTGD (alt, https://www.diigo.com/item/pdf/zk1n/juhm)

188 Umair Haque. Betterness – Economics for Humans . 2011. https://a.co/3q3Hlrv

189 Beetroot site. https://radicals.world/FVWa4r

190 Marcel Schwantes. The Job Interview Will Soon Be Dead. Here's What the Top Companies Are Replacing It with. Inc Magazine, March 2017. https://radicals.world/gp0FIy (alt, https://diigo.com/0hjgrl)

191 Marcel Schwant. The Job Interview Will Soon Be Dead. Here's What the Top Companies Are Replacing It with. Inc Magazine, March 2017. https://radicals.world/gp0FIy (alt, https://diigo.com/0hjgj8)

192 Henry George. Progress and Poverty. https://radicals.world/FlyN7j (alt, https://www.diigo.com/user/matt_perez/b/534275447)

193 Louis O Kelso and Patricia Hetter. Two-Factor Theory. 1967. https://radicals.world/tMPCZ1 (alt, https://www.diigo.com/user/matt_perez/b/525123903)

194 Originally called the Employee Stock Ownership Trust (ESOT).

195 The Kelso Institute. Important Dates In the History of Binary Economics. https://radicals.world/S40RuS

196 See Employee Retirement Income Security Act of 1974 for more references. https://radicals.world/SvMm20

197 Darren Dahl, If You Dislike Paying Taxes, You're Going to Love ESOPs. https://radicals.world/6YrXt5 (alt, https://diigo.com/0ipzub)

198 Justin Goodbread interviews Ben Wells, Pros and Cons of Selling Your Business to Employees with an ESOP. June 29, 2018. https://radicals.world/SFPuPj (alt, https://diigo.com/0ghvp4)

199 N Kurland, D Brohawn, M Greaney. Capital Homesteading for Every Citizen, p 33. https://radicals.world/NGPbZR (alt, https://diigo.com/0hfd10)

200 Nominally, they have to be US companies, but there's a way around that.

201 John Case. Capitalism for People. https://radicals.world/4mffiL (alt, https://diigo.com/0iq008)

202 David Johanson and Rachol Markun, Hawkins Parnell & Young LLP, ESOP Pros and Cons. https://radicals.world/RH9etv (alt, https://diigo.com/0h23uo)

203 The Menke Group. The Origin and History of the ESOP and Its Future Role as a Business Succession Tool. https://radicals.world/XsJrpt (alt, https://diigo.com/0iq00e)

204 For more information, see Floating Rate Notes. https://en.wikipedia.org/wiki/Floating_rate_note

205 Mel Conway, Conway's Law (PDF). https://radicals.world/IhKdW6

206 Peter Carbonara. Small Business Guide: What Owners Need to Know about Open-Book Management, Forbes Magazine. https://radicals.world/jg3a82 (alt, https://diigo.com/0gy7l8)

207 Great Game of Business. Employee Ownership. https://radicals.world/RH9etv

208 Dr Corey Rosoen. Employee Ownership (15:47) at Stanford University. June 2009. https://youtu.be/VJzZY6GLarE?t=947

209 Martin Staubus, The Effectiveness of Equity Ownership. Sep 6, 2016. https://radicals.world/PaSSBq (alt, https://diigo.

com/0h240j)

210 The original was published in the ESOP Association's ESOP Report, Sep 2019. https://radicals.world/ayHqw1 (alt, https://diigo.com/0ipzhr)

211 John Williams. The Secret to Creating an Ownership Culture: Hint—It's Not Just About Equity. You can read Why Incentive Plans Cannot Work by Alfie Kohn or watch this TED Talk by Daniel Pink, The Puzzle of Motivation. https://radicals.world/0yWeEx (alt, https://diigo.com/0h23wg) https://radicals.world/InYWQy (alt, https://www.diigo.com/item/pdf/zk1n/2r74) https://www.youtube.com/watch?time_continue=3&v=rrkrvAUbU9Y&feature=emb_logo

212 Daniel Pink. Drive: The Surprising Truth About What Motivates Us. https://radicals.world/PBx1UZ

213 Dr Corey Rosen. Employee Ownership (15:47). Stanford University, Jul 29, 2009. https://youtu.be/VJzZY6GLarE?t=947

214 2019 California Co-op Conference. https://radicals.world/RPBD3q (alt, https://diigo.com/0ipzjp)

215 The Basque Autonomous Community includes the provinces of Biscay, Gipuzkoa, and Alava. It does not include Navarra. https://radicals.world/crB1Sj https://en.wikipedia.org/wiki/Provinces_of_Spain

216 Uniform Limited Cooperative Association Act 1007 (amended 2013) [PDF]. https://radicals.world/9gIi2T (alt, https://diigo.com/0hlut1)

217 Ladislaus "Laddie" Lushin. A Trojan Horse in Our Midst: Ten faults of the Uniform Limited Cooperative Association Act. 2010. "Patrons" are the people who embody the LCA. https://radicals.world/exYCL1 (alt, https://diigo.com/0hlhgy)

218 James Dean, Thomas Earl Geu. The Uniform Limited Cooperative Association Act. 2008. https://radicals.world/oylENa (alt, https://www.diigo.com/item/pdf/zk1n/eg74#)

219 Private communications.

220 NCEO's ESOP (Employee Stock Ownership Plan) Facts. https://radicals.world/7SKlmo (alt, https://diigo.com/0ipzpu)

221 QOLiHoP, pronounced qual-ee-hop. https://radicals.world/ pCJwvF (alt, https://diigo.com/0ix2cn)

222 Anthony Matthews. Who's Who Governing ESOPs and ESOP Companies. March 2000. https://radicals.world/LXcqsd

223 James Dornbrook. Court rejects Ferrellgas ESOP trustee's request for restraining order. Nov 8, 2019. https://radicals. world/tyKsjo (alt, https://diigo.com/0ipzq3)

224 N Kurland, D Brohawn, M Greaney. Capital Homesteading for Every Citizen, p 36. https://radicals.world/NGPbZR (alt, https://diigo.com/0hfd10)

225 Dr Corey Rosen, John Case, Martin Staubus. Equity. Harvard Business Review Press, 2005. https://radicals.world/M0f5zh

226 Dr Corey Rosen. Employee Ownership (15:47). July 29, 2009. https://youtu.be/VJzZY6GLarE?t=947

227 Dr Corey Rosen. Employee Ownership (15:57). July 29, 2009. https://youtu.be/VJzZY6GLarE?t=957

228 Elinor Ostrom Facts. The Nobel Prize site. https://radicals. world/XZgUWa (alt, https://diigo.com/0iqaaf)

229 See Common Pool Resources for more references. https:// en.wikipedia.org/wiki/Common-pool_resource

230 Dr David Sloan Wilson. Prosocial World, at 2:52. https:// radicals.world/RjFDPo

231 PROSOCIAL Institute site. https://radicals.world/gPlxOI

232 Dr Paul Atkins, course material. PROSOCIAL Facilitator Certification. 2019. https://radicals.world/gPlxOI

233 Alex "Sandy" Pentland. Social Physics. 2015. https://a.co/ a43U5Xo

234 Dave Logan, et al. Tribal Leadership. 2008. https://a. co/9RSFdKF

235 Ritu Yadav. Five Eco-friendly Entrepreneurs Who Are Helping Our Environment, SheThePeople.TV, The Women's Channel. https://radicals.world/hPurnv

236 Prerna Prasad, Antara Chatterjee, Sahar Mansoor, Neerja Palisetty, Shagun Singh. https://www.linkedin.com/in/

prerna-prasad-8bb49b19/ https://www.linkedin.com/in/ antara-chatterjee-6b79a631/ https://www.linkedin.com/in/ sahar-mansoor-a6aa3623/ https://www.linkedin.com/in/ neerja-palisetty-8056508/ https://www.linkedin.com/in/ shagun-singh-161546a/

237 Nora Bateson. Symathesy: A Word in Progress . Nov 3, 2015. http://radicals.world/9PF5De (alt, https://diigo.com/0ibaxv)

238 Andrew Carnegie. Hymn to Wealth and a recording of it. https://en.wikipedia.org/wiki/Paul_Buchheit (alt, https:// diigo.com/0ibl31)

239 See Sand Hill Road and Venture Capital for more references. https://en.wikipedia.org/wiki/Sand_Hill_Road (alt, https:// en.wikipedia.org/wiki/Venture_capital)

240 See Paul Buchheit for more references. https://en.wikipedia. org/wiki/Paul_Buchheit (alt, https://diigo.com/0ibl31)

241 John R Boyd. Destruction and Creation. Sept 3, 1976. Emphasis added. https://radicals.world/7efle8 (alt, https://www.diigo. com/item/pdf/zk1n/bmtj)

242 Source, Gaeatimes; comments in Ycombinator. https://radicals. world/C7Z2wl (alt, https://diigo.com/0iwbi6) https://radicals. world/uVU0dl (alt, https://diigo.com/0iwbid)

243 Karen Southwick. High Noon, p 103. 1999. https://radicals. world/LZbnkm

244 Karen Southwick. High Noon, p 104. 1999. https://radicals. world/SOExMZ

245 For more information, see Iris Hernandez. radicals.world/ vUdbrZ

246 Pim de Morree. Morning Star's Success Story: No Bosses, No Titles, No Structural Hierarchy. 2017. https://radicals.world/ AyhAvb (alt, https://diigo.com/0ipzes)

247 Frederic Laloux. Reinventing Organizations. 2014. https:// radicals.world/g6MC0m (alt, https://diigo.com/0ipzf2)

248 See Integral Theory for more references. https://en.wikipedia. org/wiki/Integral_theory_(Ken_Wilber)

249 Steve Denning. The Leader's Guide to Radical Management. 2014. https://radicals.world/h6OP8b (alt, https://diigo.com/0ipzf8)

250 Denning's emphasis in The Leader's Guide to Radical Management. Forbes, Jan 15, 2014. https://radicals.world/h6OP8b (alt, https://diigo.com/0ipzf8)

251 We were part of a panel at the D10E Conference in San Francisco, California, on July 20, 2016. https://radicals.world/EjdRJH (alt, https://diigo.com/0ipzfn)

252 Holacracy Is Not What You Think: A Response to Steve Denning's "Making Sense of Zappos and Holacracy" by Olivier Compagne, Partner at HolacracyOne. https://radicals.world/KLSUpQ (alt, https://diigo.com/0jugpg)

253 Holon and Holarchy : Arthur Koestler. Sociocracy site, 25 June 2014. https://www.sociocracy.info/holon-and-holarchy/ (alt, https://diigo.com/0ibuuu)

254 kenwilber.com site. http://www.kenwilber.com/ (alt, https://www.diigo.com/item/pdf/zk1n/8xin#)

255 Brian Robertson. Twitter post. Jan 2, 2014. https://twitter.com/h1brian/status/418904458324488192

256 Jack Welch, General Electric's CEO, and Scott McNealy, Sun's CEO, were golf buddies and McNeally picked up this particular policy from Welch.

257 Diane Jerm quoting Vicky Saunders, founder of ShEO, in Sparking social change with feel-good investments. 2009. https://radicals.world/CmACEO https://radicals.world/qUee8z (alt, https://diigo.com/0ipz80)

258 Suzi Weissman. The Rise of Bullshit Jobs: An interview with David Graebber. June 30, 2018. Also by Graeber, On the Phenomenon of Bullshit Jobs: A Work Rant, August 2013. https://radicals.world/IfsB6P (alt, https://diigo.com/0ipz9t) https://radicals.world/aIuau2 (alt, https://diigo.com/0ipza3)

259 Andre Pusey. Beyond capitalist enclosure, commodification and alienation. Postcapitalist praxis as commons, social production and useful doing. Jan 2, 2016. https://radicals.world/IfsB6P

(alt, https://diigo.com/0ipz9t)

260 John Spedan Lewis, founder, The John Lewis Partnership. https://radicals.world/KLSw1r (alt, https://diigo.com/0ipzbf)

261 Matthew Desmond. In order to understand the brutality of American capitalism, you have to start on the plantation. Aug 14, 2019 https://radicals.world/ygTlYx (alt, https://diigo.com/0ipzbp)

262 Fredric Jameson. The Seeds of Time, p xii. 1994. https://radicals.world/CwtnRx

263 Mary Parker Follett. The New State: Group Organization [as] the Solution of Popular Government. 1918. https://a.co/6P4BS0i

264 Encyclopedia Britannica. https://www.britannica.com/topic/property-law

265 SCORE. Towards a Definition of a Consumer Stock Ownership Plan (CSOP). https://radicals.world/CEzjDW (alt, https://diigo.com/0jhqum)

266 Anne Burroughs Gilchrist, A Woman's Estimate of Walt Whitman in a letter to W M Rossetti. https://radicals.world/v1XyaA (alt, https://diigo.com/0ic4za)

267 Cooperatives call it patronage, which comes from the Latin word pater or father. So, patronage is more like the allowance that your parents give you rather than a dividend which you've earned.

268 Garry Ridge, CEO, WD-40. https://radicals.world/DfSJQG

269 Matt Perez. Bad Word of the Day: Employees. https://radicals.world/1uhA8f (alt, https://diigo.com/0ipzct)

270 Somewhat similar to what political philosopher Hanzi Freinacht calls dominator hierarchies in his book, The Listening Society. https://metamoderna.org/in-defense-of-hierarchies-amonghumans/

271 Marjorie Kelly. The Divine Right of Capital. 2003. https://radicals.world/6UCPor (alt, https://www.diigo.com/item/pdf/zk1n/pc1b)

272 Jo Freeman. The Tyranny of Structurelessness. 1970. https://radicals.world/pYrd9D (alt, https://www.jofreeman.com/joreen/tyranny.htm)

273 Dr Adrian Bejan. Freedom and Evolution: Hierarchy in Nature, Society and Science. 2020. https://a.co/98AmoMr

274 Viktor Frankl, Man's Search for Meaning, p 132.

275 In Spanish slang, a bribe is called mordida, a bite.

276 Jack Quart. Beyond the Bottom Line: Socially Innovative Business Owners. 2000. Emphasis added. https://a.co/fStDJ72

277 Raj Aggarwal and Betty J Simkins. Open Book Management-Optimizing Human Capital. Business Horizons, September-October 2001. https://radicals.world/choT24 (alt, https://www.diigo.com/user/matt_perez/b/547177300)

278 Peter Carbonara. Small Business Guide: What Owners Need to Know about Open-Book Management, Forbes Magazine. https://radicals.world/jg3a82 (alt, https://diigo.com/0gy7l8)

279 Dr Corey Rosen. Employee Ownership (15:47) at Stanford University. June 2009. https://youtu.be/VJzZY6GLarE?t=947

280 Lisa Gill pointed out that the Enspiral Handbook defines a pod which is similar in spirit to what we have in mind.

281 Many thanks to Dr Alicia Castillo for instigating this discussion that resulted in this. https://www.linkedin.com/in/aliciacastilloholley/

282 Martin Luther King Jr.'s 'Letter from Birmingham Jail. https://radicals.world/FxApMC (alt, https://diigo.com/0iicpd)

CPSIA information can be obtained
at www.ICGtesting.com
Printed in the USA
LVHW022105201122
733658LV00003B/380

9 781641 846424